The Arno Press Cinema Program

VACHEL LINDSAY:
THE POET AS FILM THEORIST

By

Glenn Joseph Wolfe

ARNO PRESS
A NEW YORK TIMES COMPANY
New York • 1973

This volume was selected for the
Dissertations on Film Series
of the ARNO PRESS CINEMA PROGRAM
by Garth S. Jowett, Carleton University

First publication in book form, Arno Press, 1973

THE ARNO PRESS CINEMA PROGRAM
For complete listing of cinema titles see last pages

Manufactured in the United States of America

- -

Library of Congress Cataloging in Publication Data

Wolfe, Glenn Joseph.
    Vachel Lindsay: the poet as film theorist.

    (The Arno Press cinema program. Dissertation on
film series)
    Originally presented as the author's thesis, State
University of Iowa, 1964.
    1. Lindsay, Nicholas Vachel, 1879-1931.
2. Moving pictures. I. Title. II. Series: The
Arno Press cinema program. III. Series: Dis-
sertations on film series.
PS3523.I58Z9 1972   814'.5'2   72-554
ISBN 0-405-04097-0

VACHEL LINDSAY: THE POET AS FILM THEORIST

by

Glenn Joseph Wolfe

A dissertation submitted in partial fulfillment of the
requirements for the degree of Doctor of Philosophy,
in the Department of Speech and Dramatic Art
in the Graduate College of the State
University of Iowa

August 1964

Chairman: Assistant Professor John B. Kuiper

ACKNOWLEDGEMENTS

I wish to thank the University of Virginia for the use of the Clifton Waller Barrett Lindsayana Collection, without which this study could not have been done. And for permission to quote from his late father's unpublished works, I sincerely thank Mr. Nicholas C. Lindsay. My appreciation is also extended to the Illinois State Historical Library for allowing me to examine its Lindsay papers. The Swarthmore College Peace Collection deserves a note of thanks for furnishing me with Vachel Lindsay's letters to Jane Addams.

To Dr. John B. Kuiper, whose encouragement, patience, and criticism have been most helpful, I extend my gratitude. My wife Judy also has offered encouragement, patience, and criticism, for which I thank her. My children, Joe, Tim, Andy and Jill have had patience, and for that I thank them.

Finally, my thanks to Mrs. Sandra Sievers for retyping the manuscript.

TABLE OF CONTENTS

INTRODUCTION

The first American to advance a theory of film was Nicholas Vachel
Lindsay (1879-1931). Although he is primarily known for his poetry, he
was the author of substantial prose works on the motion picture.[1] Because he is best known as a poet, Lindsay's theoretical writings on the
film have received little scholarly attention. His work has been given
only cursory treatment in biographies and contemporary publications.
For example, of the four dissertations concerned with Lindsay's work
only one devotes space to a hasty, yet competent, description of his
first film book, The Art of the Moving Picture. To date, no study has
been devoted to a thorough examination of Lindsay's writings on the film.
Such an investigation is long overdue and needs to be undertaken in order to help us understand American contributions to the theory of film.

Vachel Lindsay's ideas about film as they are expressed in his
books and articles, are not easily understood. They are confused by
several factors. Lindsay looked upon himself as a life-long student
of the graphic and plastic arts. For example, even when he was writing poetry he claimed to be a maker of pictures, rather than a dealer
in words. It is characteristic of Lindsay that while he practiced one
art, he consistently explained his work in terms of another art. This
ambivalence gave rise to what may be called a poet-graphic artist conflict in his writing. This conflict points up the second factor which
makes Lindsay's ideas about film difficult to understand. His theoretical notions are often hidden beneath a layer of mystical and visionary
language. In addition to these two factors, Lindsay's wide range of

interests tend to confuse a reader. He was very much concerned with religion, politics, the structure of society, and with the general welfare of his fellow man. While these interests may be the natural concerns of any creative artist and are the necessary ingredients of a theory of film which views the motion picture as an influential part of society, Lindsay confuses the reader by spending too much time exploring his own personal views of them. He quite often neglects to explore their relation to film. If we are to have an understanding of his views we must clear away the irrelevancies, the poetic flights, and the personal prejudices in order to expose the theories which lie beneath this ornate surface.

The little commentary which exists on Lindsay's film theory is either of a descriptive or critical nature. It does not attempt to go beneath the surface for an understanding of his theories. It is the purpose of this study to analyze all of Lindsay's available writings on film, both published and unpublished. Since it appears to be his most comprehensive and definitive statement on film, particular emphasis will be placed upon an examination of The Art of the Moving Picture. More specifically, this study is an explication of Lindsay's major theoretical constructs, sculpture in motion, painting in motion, architecture in motion, and hieroglyphics.[2]

Sculpture in motion, painting in motion, architecture in motion and hieroglyphics are theoretical constructs which run through all of Lindsay's writings on film. Together they constitute a single strand of thought which permeates his books, lectures, essays, correspondence, and personal notebooks. For example, hieroglyphics is a construct

which appears regardless of what Lindsay may be writing about--
art, poetry, film, etc. From these four constructs Lindsay derived
criteria for the motion picture as an art form. In a word, these constructs are guides to the way the motion picture is organized. Equally
important to this investigation is the reason for Lindsay's interest
in the way film functions as a structural entity. Thus the study also
analyzes the way in which Lindsay's structural theories relate to his
views on art, religion, aesthetics, and the social milieu.

The reader will note that the study has two distinct parts. Except for Chapter I which is an introductory survey of Lindsay's writing
on film, the study is divided into social factors and structural
theories. This two-part division follows the organization of Lindsay's
writings.

Part I of the study deals with Lindsay's social views, his ideas
about art, and his religious convictions. Chapter II outlines what
Lindsay identified as the social problems of the day, his reactions to
these problems, and the ways he proposed that society could use the
film to combat them. The third chapter deals with Lindsay's general
view of art, his view of art as a part of society, and the way in which
he perceived the art of the film as a means to improve society. Chapter
IV is an examination of the relationships which Lindsay saw among beauty,
art, and religion. In addition, Chapter IV examines the way in which
these relationships can improve film, and thus improve society. It will
be noticed that Part I of the study proceeds from the general to the
specific inasmuch as Chapter II outlines what Lindsay takes to be the
problems of society, while Chapters III and IV discuss his specific

suggestions as to how film may improve the society in which it exists.

Part II of the study analyzes Lindsay's structural theory of the film. The purpose of the chapters which cover the "motion" concepts is to clarify and analyze precisely what Lindsay attempted to do when he applied terms from the traditional arts to the film. Chapter V is devoted to an examination of the plastic elements of sculpture and how they are related to the illusion of depth in the motion picture. The chapter entitled "Painting in Motion" describes Lindsay's theories of two-dimensional composition and his treatment of filmic time and space. In Chapter VII the emphasis is on the anthropomorphic propensities of the film and the way in which film is able to deal with scenes of monumental proportions. The chapter on "Hieroglyphics" is an exami-nation of Lindsay's theory of symbolism.

In the discussion chapter the two parts of the study are drawn to-gether in order to demonstrate the relationships which exist between Lindsay's social and structural theories. In the process, Lindsay's views on art and society are examined in the context of his time. Furthermore, attention is given to the way in which Lindsay's ideas on art and society resemble the views of his contemporaries in literature and art. Finally, Lindsay's film theory is placed in perspective by comparing his ideas with those of other early theorists and by demon-strating the way his ideas have been brought to fruition by later theorists.

NOTES

[1]Lindsay's published works include The Art of the Moving Picture (1915), four movie reviews for The New Republic (1917), a short article in Moving Picture World of 1917, and an article on Douglas Fairbanks published in The Ladies Home Journal of 1926. His unpublished works include "The Greatest Movies Now Running" (1925) which is a second full-length prose work, essays on film, and innumerable references to film in his personal diaries, notes, and correspondence. The extent and nature of Lindsay's writings on film is surveyed in more detail in Chapter I.

[2]The term theoretical construct refers to a network of ideas. Lindsay constructs such a network and gives each a specific name (i.e., sculpture in motion, painting in motion, architecture in motion, and hieroglyphics.).

PART I

SOME INFLUENTIAL FACTORS

CHAPTER I

A Survey of Film Materials

In order to acquaint the reader with Lindsay's writings on film
and to indicate the function and scope of some of the materials upon
which the study will draw, this chapter surveys Lindsay's published
and unpublished works. This survey treats only Lindsay's writings on
the film and is not intended as an exhaustive description of every
source used in the study.

The Art of the Moving Picture

While Lindsay's work, The Art of the Moving Picture,[1] does not
stand as the sole film book of the period, it appears to be the first
full length work devoted to serious thought about what film as an art
form should be, what it should do, and how it should do it. In other
words, Lindsay was the first American to theorize about the film. The
plurality of other works produced prior to 1915, were concerned with
furnishing helpful hints on how to make a living in the movie industry,
how to act for the movies, how to write photoplays, and general information about how the movies are made. Lindsay's work, by contrast,
stands alone as a treatment of the aesthetic potentialities of the film,
of its future as an individual art form, and of its social mission.

In terms of internal reference, there is little in The Art of the
Moving Picture that tells the reader how Lindsay approached his work.
However, he does provide some statements about his methodology. For
example, he states that the book was written from an "artistic" bias.

To use his words:

> Throughout this book I try to bring to bear the same simple
> standards of form, composition, mood, and motive that we
> used in finding the fundamental exhibits; the standards which
> are taken for granted in art histories and schools, radical
> or conservative anywhere.[2]

A check of the book's table of contents reveals that Lindsay drew
heavily on his training and interest in the graphic and plastic arts.
We find, for instance, that three of his theoretical constructs are
called painting, sculpture, and architecture in motion. Another indication of Lindsay's "artistic" bias can be found in his contention
that the effects of the film are closely related to those produced by
fine gallery painting and sculpture. Such effects occur, Lindsay says,
even though the apparent emphasis of the film is on dramatic structure.
In short, he contends that the final effect of the film is "the spirit
of Tintoretto rather than that of Moliere."[3] That Lindsay would hold
such an opinion is not suprising in view of his fondness for pictorial
beauty in any form. However, Lindsay was not interested in merely
comparing the film with what he considered to be the finest examples of
the established arts. Rather, he was trying to find something of artistic worth in the film; something that would show the world that the film
truly was worthy of acceptance as a new and vital art form. As he puts
it: "This book tries to find that fourth dimension of architecture,
painting, and sculpture, which is the human soul in action, that arrow
with wings which is the flash of fire from the film, or the heart of
man. . . ."[4]

One of Lindsay's more prevalent ideas about his own work is the

fact that he insists upon refering to it as a critical work, one designed as an aid in classifying and judging motion pictures. In fact, as a
result of either a finely-honed sense of humor or a complete lack of
modesty, Lindsay refers to Book II of the 1922 edition of The Art of the
Moving Picture, as "The Unchallenged Outline of Photoplay Critical
Method."[5] Although Lindsay calls his work one of criticism and judgement,
he is certainly aware of the fine line between criticism and theory. He
is aware that one cannot criticize sensibly without first establishing
some theoretical notions. Even though Lindsay calls it a critical work,
it is neither unfair nor inaccurate to refer to the work as a theoretical
one. This is true because a great portion of the book is devoted to
speculation about what the film should be, what it should do, and to a
discussion of the techniques for establishing it as a reputable art form.

Lindsay's notion about the audience for whom he wrote The Art of
the Moving Picture is a confused one. The opening sentence of the 1915
edition states that the book is "primarily for photoplay audiences."[6]
But Lindsay continues by saying that he also desires the work to have
some effect on those people who are in the business of actually making
films. The important fact is, though, that Lindsay truly wished for a
critical film audience made up of all strata of society. To his way of
thinking, film was the most powerful and comprehensive means of communication since the development of the printing press. He reasoned
that to encourage the development of film as an art he must encourage
the average moviegoer to develop a critical sense. There can be little
doubt that Lindsay had this in mind as he wrote The Art of the Moving

<u>Picture</u>. Unfortunately the book proved a bit too mystical, and in some cases, a bit too scholarly to be of use to the average moviegoer of 1915. Lindsay seemed to have realized this. In the second edition he states:

> While there is a great deal of literary reference in all the following argument, I realize, looking back over many attempts to paraphrase it for various audiences, that its appeal is to those who spend the best part of their student life in classifying, and judging, and producing works of sculpture, painting, and architecture. I find the eyes of all others wandering when I make talks upon the plastic artist's point of view.[7]

Although Lindsay freely admitted the shortcomings of his work insofar as its appeal to the common man was concerned, the book nevertheless held some appeal for a least a limited segment of the population. It was reprinted in 1916 and a second edition was brought out in 1922.[8]

Lindsay's own evaluation of <u>The Art of the Moving Picture</u> as it appears in the book itself indicates that the work was one whose substructure was definitely from the world of graphic arts. It grew from a desire to construct a critical system for the average moviegoer. Lindsay hoped to provide a method to enable a viewer to "judge and classify" the pictures he saw.

Before turning to Lindsay's external references to the book, it might be well to note the way in which the book was advertised by its publisher, the Macmillan Company. In a promotional flyer which purports to be the work of the publisher, we find <u>The Art of the Moving Picture</u> advertised as "an effort to apply the Gospel of Beauty to a new art."[9] In sharp contrast to this honest portrayal of the book stands a passage written by the agency which acted as manager for one of Lindsay's lecture tours:

> Mr. Lindsay considers the double citation of <u>The Art of the Moving Picture</u>, in the Brittanica, his greatest and most substantial honor from the world of scholarship and science. to have been a surviving pioneer in so highly technical and complicated a field as the movies, and to have been able to transfer his ten years of art museum study into so modern a field, under such terrific critical scrutiny, and amid such continued confusion as is essential to Hollywood, is evidence of some saving remnant of critical force in the book.[10]

There are elements of truth in both of these promotional pieces; however, the last one is more typical of the hyperbolic statement expected from a publicist rather than a straightforward evaluation of the worth of the book itself.

Lindsay's other writing contains many references to <u>The Art of the Moving Picture</u>. In them he stresses that the book is based on his training in art. As he puts it:

> I based my movie study on four years of working out the theory of sculpture, architecture, painting and landscape gardening in the library of the Chicago Art Institute and in the Museum, and four years of similar study in the Metropolitan Museum, New York. Pardon my modesty. I must present my credentials.[11]

Lindsay was never one to be bothered by false modesty when it came to writing about his work on the film. He is never remiss to state that his was the first serious study of the film and that some of the books which followed used <u>The Art of the Moving Picture</u> as a foundation.[12] Worthy of note, too, is the fact that Lindsay took to poetry to explain his film writing. In the following verse we see him looking at his writing and his plans for future works on the film:

> In nineteen hundred and
> Fifteen
> When I was thirty-five
> I wrote my book on the movies

As I watched them come alive.
In nineteen hundred and twenty-one
When I was forty-one
I revised my book on the
Movies
Testing good works done
Along the lines I hope for.
In nineteen forty-four
I will revise my movie book
And praise new work some
More. 13

The Influence of The Art of the Moving Picture

Assessment of the actual influence of Lindsay's work on the film

community or the general populace can be, at best, only speculatory.

However, speculation based on Lindsay's own comments about the influ-

ence of the book does suggest the extent of its influence. For ex-

ample, in "The Greatest Movies Now Running," Lindsay has this to say of

The Art of the Moving Picture:

> The author of this book wrote The Art of the Moving Picture
> in 1914. It was first published in 1915. It became the
> textbook for the photoplay classes of the Columbia University
> School of Journalism, and, if I may here put down a boast, it
> was the first textbook on the movies ever used in any uni-
> versity in the world. Victor O. Freeburg conducted the class-
> es with the book for the basis of his teaching, then evolved
> his book, The Art of Photoplay Writing, from his lectures to
> that class. . . . Meanwhile I became the photoplay editor of
> The New Republic, wrote very elaborate reviews of many of
> the productions of that time. . . . I find now the standard
> motion picture critics using every day the standards of
> judgment and the dogmas set up by my precious book.14

Lindsay was extremely proud of the fact that his book was adopted as a

text for a film course at Columbia University. This pride is evidenced

by his propensity for mentioning the fact on many occasions. In a 1917

letter to Harriet Monroe, Lindsay states that the book "has been

accepted by the Columbia University Scenario Class."15 Eight years

later, Lindsay was still mentioning the fact that his book had received
use in the university; however, now he attributes considerable more influence to the book:

> The original Art of the Moving Picture. . . was the first
> textbook used by any university anywhere, in regard to the
> films. It was the basis of Victor O. Freeburg's classes
> in photoplay writing which were conducted in the Columbia
> University School of Journalism from 1915 through to about
> 1917, by Freeburg, and are continued, so far as I know, to
> this day. Freeburg wrote a textbook afterwards. . . .
> based on mine, and due credit is given in the preface.[16]

The best justification for saying that any comment on the actual in-

fluence of Lindsay's book must be speculatory is that Lindsay had

trouble keeping his facts straight and at times appears to attribute

more influence to the book than it actually had. A case in point is

the instance just cited, Dr. Freeburg's use of the book in his classes

at Columbia. The facts appear to be these: First of all, the Freeburg

work to which Lindsay refers as having been influenced by The Art of the

Moving Picture is not entitled The Art of Photoplay Writing. Its true

title is The Art of Photo-Play Making.[17] Secondly, if in fact Freeburg's

work was, as Lindsay puts it, "based on" The Art of the Moving Picture,

"due credit" is hardly given to Lindsay in the preface. Freeburg says

that one of the three books which the readers should have "at hand and

open" is Lindsay's Art of the Moving Picture. He then gives the follow-

ing brief characterization of Lindsay's work: "[The Book] makes it per-

fectly clear that a motion picture, if properly thought out and manu-

factured, will contain the kind of beauty which we used to look for

only in painting and sculpture."[18] If this is "due credit" Lindsay

was easily satisfied It is conceivable that Lindsay was refering to

Freeburg's later work on the film; however, a check of the preface of
this work characterizes The Art of the Moving Picture only as a pioneer
work "in which the pictorial art of the screen has been appraised without analysis. . . ."[19]

Another of Lindsay's contemporaries, Hugo Munsterberg, was aware
of The Art of the Moving Picture, and apparently was acquainted with
Lindsay himself. Munsterberg, best known as a psychologist, was himself a student of the film and published his own observations on the
subject just one year after Lindsay's work appeared.[20] A year later,
while serving as a movie reviewer for The New Republic, Lindsay wrote a
review of Munsterberg's book, in which he decried the fact that Munsterberg's book "has been elaborately praised, but complete ignored by the
professional photoplay critics of the big newspapers."[21] Lindsay's
point was that there was a great deal in Munsterberg's book which de-
served serious attention. It should be noted, however, that Lindsay
used the review largely as a vehicle for exposing his own theoretical
ideas rather than Munsterberg's. Thus the review gives a reader little
information as to what Lindsay believed were the strengths and weak-
nesses of Munsterberg's book.

It is unclear as to whether or not Lindsay's writings on film had
any direct influence on Munsterberg's book. Lindsay saw similarities
between his own work and Munsterberg's, yet he insisted that these
similarities were fortuitous. As he put it:

> Munsterberg has the best book on the scientific side I think,
> and the bridge between us can be found in the phrase I have
> italicized and its implications 'space measured without sound,
> plus time measured without sound.' I am delighted to have so

much common ground with Munsterberg. His book appeared
several months after mine and we worked quite independ-
ently.[22]

Furthermore, it is evident from this statement that Lindsay was pleased

with the similarities between the two books, and looked upon Munster-

berg's work with considerable favor. However, about ten years later

the situation had changed. In "The Greatest Movies Now Running" Lind-

say characterized Munsterberg's book as "all science and prophecy and

aside from the italicized portions, [one which] purported to be

nothing but a journalistic excursion."[23] This change in viewpoint is

indeed perplexing in view of the fact that Lindsay had exchanged

correspondence with Munsterberg about the film, and had been generally

favorable in his review of The Photo-Play.[24]

The effect of The Art of the Moving Picture on the film industry,

if indeed it had any effect, is not documented by film historians or

journalists of Lindsay's time. However, Lindsay's own assessment of the

effect his book had on people in the industry is available. Lindsay

possessed an almost child-like admiration for some of the so-called

Hollywood "stars." So strong was this admiration that he wrote poetry

about movies and the people in them.[25] Two of Lindsay's favorite movie

personalities were Mary Pickford and Douglas Fairbanks, both of them he

saw as persons to be emulated by the average moviegoer. Lindsay was

able to arrange discussions about the movies with Pickford and Fairbanks.

On at least one occasion he was their guest in California. Apparently

Lindsay took this opportunity to offer them his books. Miss Pickford

replied to his gift in these words:

I cannot tell you how glad I am to have the copies of your
books. I had read some of them, of course; in fact both
Douglas and I have long been your admirers, but since that
enjoyable day at the studio, I shall read them with a new
interest and a new understanding.[26]

There is evidence to indicate that The Art of the Moving Picture was

also respected and admired by at least one film writer.[27] Furthermore

it appears that Lindsay took it upon himself to distribute copies of the

book within the movie colony. Included among his personal papers is a

note in Lindsay's hand indicating that books were given to Dan Frohman,

a theatrical producer and backer of Hollywood's Famous Players Company,

Ralph Ince, an early film director and actor, and Leonard Dyer,

described by Lindsay as "Edison's man."[28]

There also appears to have been considerable interest in the book

by people outside the movie industry. Jane Addams was interested in the

work Lindsay was doing. On two separate occasions Lindsay expressed his

appreciation to Miss Addams for "backing" The Art of the Moving Picture.[29]

According to Lindsay, Gordon Craig also admired the book. Lindsay

characterized Craig's interest in it as follows: "Gordon Craig wrote me

a year ago (after reading my book) that if I would give the word, he

would come to America at once and start a photoplay studio with me. He

seemed to accept the whole volume."[30]

There is little doubt that Lindsay admired David Wark Griffith

above all other persons in the motion picture business. His admiration

for Griffith's work is illustrated by the following comment:

I wrote a whole book about Griffith once. It was called The
Art of the Moving Picture. . . . When it came to looking up
the director and prime mover in all the films I considered
worth mentioning in both issues of that book, I found that

Griffith had done them all. I said as much in the book. . . . Griffith is the great genius of the movies and will be forevermore.[31]

Beyond his admiration for Griffith's work, there remains the question of what influence, if any, Lindsay's book may have had on Griffith. Lindsay's personal papers are filled with allusions to Griffith which purport to document the admiration Griffith had for The Art of the Moving Picture. However, it is impossible to verify Lindsay's comments from other sources. The D. W. Griffith Collection at the Museum of Modern Art contains no correspondence relating to Lindsay.[32] In other words, we must rely only on Lindsay for information pertaining to the connection between the two men, and for information about how The Art of the Moving Picture may have affected Griffith. According to the reports contained in Lindsay's personal correspondence, Griffith was familar with the work, and expressed considerable admiration for the book. One of Lindsay's earliest references to Griffith occurs in a letter written while he was the motion picture critic for The New Republic. Lindsay says:

Did you know that the great Griffith telegraphed for me to go to New York and return at his expense to witness the performance of Intolerance! I boast of it blatantly. It means I am getting some where as a motion picture critic.[33]

A short while later Lindsay wrote another friend about Griffith's acceptance of The Art of the Moving Picture:

People in the commercial end of the business consider the last section of the book where the people around you would approve-- they consider the last sections mere moon-talk. Griffith and Sargent are polite enough to let me take them to school as it were, but not to church.[34]

The section of the book which Lindsay calls "moon-talk" refers to the last part of it. There Lindsay sets down his ideas about the future of the film as a means of cultural and spiritual salvation. Apparently the practical men of Hollywood were interested in Lindsay's theories but not in his sermons. In the quote above, for instance, Lindsay admits that Griffith was not in sympathy with the sermonizing in the book. On the other hand, Lindsay insists that Griffith characterized The Art of the Moving Picture as generally "the most beautiful book on the subject ever written."[35] In his letters and with characteristic pride, Lindsay intimates that the people within the movie industry who read his book found the first half, the theoretical section, quite understandable. But Lindsay is forced to admit that people outside the industry were apt to find his theories "daring."[36] In addition to Griffith's fondness for the theories contained in The Art of the Moving Picture, Lindsay tells us that Griffith attempted to make the work better known among his cohorts in the movie industry. He reported that Griffith distributed one hundred copies to members of his studio.[37] Eight years later however, Lindsay revised the estimate:

> Griffith put fifty copies of my book in his studios before he began to plan Intolerance. If I should insist that the book influenced Intolerance, the motion picture way of receiving that would be that I will begin to demand back salary. We must cure them of this. I am entirely too vain to allow any such point of view to exist in my presence. I really value honor, the purely abstract literary and esthetic honor, of having written the first book on the motion picture and of disarming these people till they will testify to my exact influence as an abstract student of esthetics in their purely esthetic moments.[38]

If we may accept his own word, it appears that Lindsay and his book were known and respected by some of the most important people in the film industry. It is difficult to document the degree to which

Lindsay's ideas were accepted or for that matter, put into practice. If
some of the films which followed Lindsay's work exhibited certain similarities to the ideas which he propounded, it is tenable that these
similarities were simply fortuitous ones. For instance, Griffith's
Birth of a Nation, the film which Lindsay often cited as an illustration
of his theoretical notions, was released nine months before Lindsay's
book reached the public eye. Therefore it is possible that later film
makers simply capitalized on the techniques developed by Griffith rather
than developing techniques based upon Lindsay's theoretical precepts.

Reviews of The Art of the Moving Picture

Contemporary critical appraisal of Lindsay's book was generally
favorable. The earliest review, published in the magazine that later
hired Lindsay as a movie critic, had this to say of his book:

> Vachel Lindsay has undertaken the fundamental brainwork necessary
> to an understanding of the moving picture art. He has done his
> heroic best to bring order out of aesthetic muddle and bewilder-
> ment. He has articulated a theory of beauty on the basis of the
> photoplay as we know it. . . . No one could be inhospitable to a
> book so vigorous and creative and fertile. It goes. . . to the
> root of the matter. It reveals vividly where the limitations
> and the opportunities of the moving picture lie. There is nothing
> fanciful about it. There is nothing chimerical. It states and
> argues its position, and opens up the hope for beauty in a form
> of expression that has been enormously misunderstood. There will
> be many, even, [sic] to halt superciliously at the very con-
> junction of the moving picture and art. But Mr. Lindsay need not
> care. He has initiated photoplay criticism.39

Another review written about a year after the publication of the book,
was not nearly so flowery as The New Republic's and yet it probably came
closer to an objection evaluation of Lindsay's work. It said of the
words: "Much of his book is discursive and consequently inconclusive,
but the part containing his thesis is lucid and suggestive and

admirably definite in its theoretical intention."[40] An interesting facet of these reviews in that both of them refer to The Art of the Moving Picture as a book of movie criticism. Apparently both reviewers took Lindsay at his word. It may well be that Lindsay viewed his book as one of criticism and yet it is debatable if the average moviegoer could have constructed a critical system for The Art of the Moving Picture.

Perhaps a growing awareness of film literature caused Lindsay's work to receive more critical attention in later years than immediately following its publication. A dozen years later Ernest Betts, while decrying a lack of film literature and criticism, cited Lindsay's work as one of the few serious attempts that had been made along these lines. He called The Art of the Moving Picture a work of imagination which "strikes out many illuminating ideas from the unformed mass of film precept and practice."[41] Another commentator saw the work as marred by eccentricities, but nevertheless the "first philosophical study of the cinema."[42] Still another, writing over two decades later epitomized the work as follows:

> Lindsay's style, florid, gossipy, always enthusiastic and often poetically rhetorical, is a mask behind which his constant perceptiveness operates. The book is full of enormous irrelevancies, long illustrations which illuminate his own meaning for himself but obscure the issues he is trying to prove at a period when virtually no one had begun to express his ideas on paper. He is not easy to quote because he seldom summarizes his position; the significance of what he is saying emerges during the course of his long and fluent paragraphs.[43]

One of the latest reviewers takes note of the highly prophetic tone of the work in addition to re-emphasizing the fact that Lindsay's book was the first of its kind to come from so respected a man of letters.[44]

The Greatest Movies Now Running

Lindsay's second major film work, "The Greatest Movies Now Running,"
unlike his first, does not propose to add anything original in the realm
of either film theory or criticism. Rather, as both external and internal evidence indicate, the book was meant to be a continuation of
the ideas put forth in The Art of the Moving Picture. Steadfast in the
hope that his pronouncements on film would be read not only by the film
critic or the film scholar but by the common man as well, Lindsay
stated in his prologue: "I have tried to write my work as seriously as
the Ten Commandments, but I want it read if possible, by every High
School kid in America, with his mouth full of Wrigley's Doublemint chew-
ing gum."[45] Not only did Lindsay continue to hope for wide readership
among the masses, he wanted the reader of the new work to look back to
The Art of the Moving Picture and there remind himself of the tenets
upon which the second work was based.[46] Lindsay's credo for the new
book is best summarized in a statement which recurs throughout the book:
"This book is based on our changing sense of what is worth hearing and
what is worth seeing, of what is worth talking about, of what is worth
praising, admiring, and adoring."[47]

Evidence from outside the work itself indicates that Lindsay was
deeply concerned about how the new book would be received. In a 1922
notebook he indicates a poet's concern as to how he might best present
the material of the new book.[48] During the writing of the book itself
his correspondence shows that he looked upon "The Greatest Movies Now
Running" as another attempt to convert some of the people in Hollywood
to his way of thinking:

> I am going at the whole battle again in my new book, and I
> most earnestly urge your cooperation in any way that occurs
> to you. We will go down there first, last and always as
> students of poetry, bring these people all the way to the
> shrine of poetry, and get them to leave behind box office
> considerations for an hour a day.[49]

As was pointed out earlier, Lindsay did not pretend that "The Greatest

Movies Now Running" presented any new theories about the film. Rather,

the new book was simply a reapplication of "all of the old doctrines of

the first textbook" to a new set of films.[50] Furthermore this re-

application of "old doctrines" to new films was only the first book

in what Lindsay visualized as continuing series:

> I have just dictated a book on the movies of 1924-25, which
> will make a year book, like Burns Mantle's yearbook of the
> stage, O'Brien's yearbook of the short story, Braithwaite's
> yearbook of poetry, or any other yearbook you may care to
> name. . . . It is far more popular and journalistic in manner,
> being dictated with a very light heart, than anything I have
> ever submitted to the public. It may mean a vast new field
> for me. No one seems to be taking this matter of the movie
> yearbook in hand.[51]

In summary then, Lindsay's second and last work on the film pro-

poses nothing strikingly new. It is, as the author admits, a re-

statement of theoretical concepts proposed some ten years earlier in

The Art of the Moving Picture; theoretical concepts which are reapplied

to a new set of films in an effort to further the notion that the films

of 1924-1925, like those of 1915, still represent the characteristics of

sculpture in motion, painting in motion, and architecture in motion.

Its value lies in the fact that it gives new examples, and in some cases,

outlines in much clearer language, the theoretical ideas of The Art of

the Moving Picture.

Lindsay's Movie Reviews

Lindsay served as a movie critic for The New Republic magazine.

His job however, was of short duration. He published only four reviews, all of them in 1917.[52] Perhaps the most striking thing about
his movie reviews is that they represent, as Scouffas has suggested,
some of Lindsay's best prose--"clear, humorous, rather deft."[53] An
analysis of Lindsay's movie criticism reveals three important points.
First, while Lindsay is writing as a critic, he is also writing as a
theorist. More precisely, he enlarges and clarifies his theory by
means of criticism. Secondly, what this writer has chosen to call
theoretical concepts are employed in Lindday's criticisms as "classifications of photoplay elements." This leads one to question whether
theory grew out of criticism or criticism from theory. Finally, the
application of his theory to a given film is severely compartmentialized.
That is, Lindsay the critic approaches each film with a point of view
derived from one of his theoretical concepts. For instance, one film
may be criticized on the basis of painting in motion, another one the
basis of sculpture in motion, and still another on the basis of hieroglyphics. Viewed as a whole Lindsay's theory and criticism add credence
to the truism that theory and criticism are inseparable.

Miscellaneous Film Material

In addition to his writings on the film, Lindsay spent some time
lecturing on the subject. Available evidence suggests that his film
lectures were offered through his agent, and were often presented along
with a performance of his poetry.[54] In a publicity flyer written by
Lindsay and entitled "A Letter About My Four Programmes" we find the
following entry:

> Programme II: A talk on the Art of the Moving Picture. An
> hour or an hour and a quarter as required. This will in-
> clude some of the verses of Programme I. For good citizen-
> ship leagues, civic committes, etc. . . . . For the speaker
> chalk and a small blackboard should be provided with a
> pointer, and room to walk in front of the blackboard.
> Several diagrams of theoretical photoplays will be made.
> Recent books on the motion picture will be discussed.[55]

A promotional sheet issued by Mrs. Lindsay while she served as her

husband's manager from 1925 to 1929, lists the following subjects

covered in Lindsay's Movie Lectures: "The Significance of the Zukor

Prize and its winner (Sabatini)"; "Photoplays of Intimacy, Action, and

Splendor"; "The Picture of the Year Analyzed (The Thief of Bagdad)";

"Aristocracy in the Movies"; "Democracy in the Movies"; and "The Movie

and World Peace." A note appended to this list states: "Illustrations

will be drawn from the best current films. Frequently Mr. Lindsay will

read from his own verse, apropos of points made as part of his lecture."[56]

In addition to the lectures mentioned above, a publicity flyer released

by the agency which assumed managership in 1929 indicates that the

following lectures were also available: "David Wark Griffith, Charles

Chaplin and Douglas Fairbanks as International Figures"; "The Talkies

versus the Moving Picture"; "The Best Movies I have Ever Seen"; and

"Painting, Sculpture, and Architecture in Motion."[57] In short, it would

appear that Lindsay's lecture material covered almost exclusively those

topics which had been treated in either The Art of the Moving Picture

or "The Greatest Movies Now Running."

Beyond the two major books, the four movie reviews, and the lecture

tours, Lindsay's extant writing on the film contain miscellaneous essays

which were not published. Among these unpublished papers is an essay

entitled "A Special Delivery Letter to My Particular Friends" which a note in Lindsay's hand describes as an editorial for the London Mercury. However, a check of that publication for the years 1925 and 1930 reveals that no such editorial appeared. The article itself is a rather polemic piece. In it Lindsay issues a diatribe against the "movie magnate" who has prostituted the American film, endorses a form of stringent censorship, and pleads for the acceptance of the film as a respectable art form.[58] Another manuscript which is included in Lindsay's personal papers is a series of short essays under the general title The Vitaphone.[59] These essays grapple with the problem of the sound film. Lindsay's position is that if the talkie is to be successful, sound must be subordinated to the picture. Aside from numerous allusions to the film in his personal correspondence, the only other work related directly to film is a manuscript of an article on Douglas Fairbanks which appeared in the Ladies Home Journal.[60]

Viewed as a unit, Lindsay's utterances on film are amazingly consistent in their general approach. The tenets which Lindsay established in his 1915 work are basis for all that follows. Painting, sculpture, architecture and hieroglyphics are followed throughout as guidelines for the isolation of particular formative elements in the film and as standards of judgement by which a critical system is established.

Important also is the reason for Lindsay's interest in the way the motion picture functions as a structural unity. Lindsay's structural theories are related to his views on art, religion, aesthetics, and the social milieu. The three chapters which follow will examine Lindsay's social views, his ideas about art, and his religious and aesthetic convictions.

NOTES

[1]Vachel Lindsay, The Art of the Moving Picture (New York: The Macmillan Company, 1915). Lindsay's book was reprinted in 1916 and a second edition was released in 1922. This slightly expanded version of The Art of the Moving Picture contains an introduction by George W. Eggers, the Director of the Denver Art Association, Lindsay's assessment of the situation of film in America, and a revised Chapter One which outlines the author's "point of view." These additions in no way change the content of the book, but serve to update the work from the viewpoint of both the author and the reader. Unless noted otherwise, all future references to The Art of the Moving Picture will be to the 1915 edition. However, in the following sequence of footnotes (through n. 7) it will be noted that the writer has distinguished between the 1915 and the 1922 edition each time an entry occurs, in an effort to avoid confusion.

[2]Ibid., (1922), p. 19.

[3]Ibid., (1915), p. 4.

[4]Ibid., (1922), p. 1.

[5]Ibid.

[6]Ibid., (1915), p. 1.

[7]Ibid., (1922), p. 1.

[8]This writer has been able to uncover only one bit of concrete evidence as to the success of the book in later years. A royalty statement for 1924 indicates sixty-seven copies sold. "Annual Statement of Royalty Account" The Macmillan Company, July 29, 1924, from the Clifton Waller Barrett Library Lindsayana Collection of the University of Virginia. Nearly all subsequent manuscript materials used in this study are from the Clifton Waller Barrett Lindsayana Collection, which will be cited hereafter as Barrett Collection.

[9]From a promotional flyer published by the Macmillan Company, n. d., Barrett Collection.

[10]From flyer entitled "About Vachel Lindsay's books" published by William B. Feakins, Inc., n. d., Barrett Collection.

[11]Vachel Lindsay, "Sound is the Servant--Not the Master of the Camera" (typescript, Barrett Collection, n. d.). Lindsay lists this short essay as an "editorial for the London Mercury." However, a check of the years 1925 through 1930 reveals no such editorial.

[12]Vachel Lindsay, "The Greatest Movies Now Running" (unpublished manuscript, Barrett Collection, n. d.), p. 8. Although the manuscript is undated, allusions in Lindsay's correspondence indicate that it was completed in 1925. A note written by Mrs. Lindsay and placed in the file which contains the manuscript says that "The Greatest Movies Now Running" was submitted to the Macmillan Company for publication in 1926, but was rejected. The book itself will be described in some detail later in this chapter.

[13]From a personal notebook, June 2, 1924, Barrett Collection.

[14]Lindsay, "The Greatest. . . ," Barrett Collection, p. 8.

[15]Letter to Harriet Monroe, January 12, 1917, quoted in Radford B. Kuydendall, "The Reading and Speaking of Vachel Lindsay" (unpublished Ph. D. dissertation, Northwestern University, 1952), p. 27.

[16]Letter to Professor Harold L. Bruce, January 17, 1925, Barrett Collection.

[17]Victor O. Freeburg, The Art of Photo-Play Making (New York: The Macmillan Company, 1918).

[18]Ibid., p. ii.

[19]Victor O. Freeburg, Pictorial Beauty on the Screen (New York: The Macmillan Company, 1923), p. ix.

[20]Hugo Munsterberg, The Photoplay: A Psychological Study (New York: D. Appleton and Company, 1916).

[21]Vachel Lindsay, "Photoplay Progress," The New Republic, 10, (February 17, 1917), pp. 76-7.

[22]Letter to Jane Addams, October 15, 1916, in Jane Addams Collection (Swarthmore College Peace Collection, Swarthmore, Pa.).

[23]Lindsay, "The Greatest. . . ," p. 107.

[24]Lindsay, The New Republic, 10, pp. 76-7.

[25]For a source which recounts Lindsay's admiration for both Mae Marsh and Anita Loos, see Anita Loos, "Vachel, Mae, and I," Saturday Review (August 26, 1961). For poems about movie personalities, see Vachel Lindsay, Collected Poems (New York: The Macmillan Company, 1925).

[26] Letter from Mary Pickford, September 10, 1924, Barrett Collection.

[27] Lindsay says: "Technically it has been accepted by the most exacting and authoritative commercial oracle on scenarios Epes Winthrop Sargeant." Letter to Harriet Monroe, January 12, 1917, quoted in Kuykendall, "The Reading. . .," p. 27.

[28] From a personal notebook, n. d., Barrett Collection. The "Leonard Dyer" of whom Lindsay speaks is probably Frank Lewis Dyer, Chief counsel for the Edison organization.

[29] Letters to Jane Addams, October 13, 1916 and October 29, 1916, Swarthmore College Peace Collection.

[30] Letter to Harriet Monroe, January 12, 1917, quoted in Kuykendall, "The Reading. . .," p. 27.

[31] Vachel Lindsay, "Why I think Douglas Fairbanks is a Great Man," manuscript, Barrett Collection, 1926, pp. 7-8.

[32] Letter from Eileen Bowser, February 24, 1964.

[33] Letter to Harriet Monroe, October 12, 1916, quoted in Kuykendall, "The Reading. . .," p. 27. Such an invitation loses its luster when one considers the possibility that all critics may have been invited in order to increase publicity.

[34] Letter to Jane Addams, October 29, 1916, Swarthmore College Peace Collection. The "Sargent" to whom Lindsay refers is Epes Winthrop Sargeant.

[35] Letter to Harriet Monroe, January 12, 1917, quoted in Kuykendall, "The Reading. . .," p. 27.

[36] Ibid.

[37] Ibid.

[38] Letter to Professor Harold L. Bruce, January 17, 1925, Barrett Collection.

[39] Francis Hackett, "The Poet at the Movies." The New Republic, V (December 25, 1915), pp. 201-2.

[40]H-M Luquiens, "The Art of the Moving Picture," The Yale Review, V (July 1916), p. 896.

[41]Ernest Betts, "The Film as Literature," Saturday Review [London] 144 (December 31, 1927), p. 905.

[42]Edgar Holt, "Vachel Lindsay, Poet and Pioneer of Cinema," Bookman [London] VII (January 1932), p. 244.

[43]Roger Manvell, "A Forgotten Critic," Sight and Sound (Spring and Winter 1949-1950), p. 76.

[44]"Vachel Lindsay on Film," Image II (April 1953), p. 23.

[45]Lindsay, "The Greatest. . .," Barrett Collection, p. iii.

[46]Ibid., p. 9.

[47]Ibid., p. 66.

[48]Personal notebook, February 26, 1922, Barrett Collection.

[49]Letter to Professor Harold L. Bruce, January 17, 1925, Barrett Collection.

[50]Ibid.

[51]Letter to Henry S. Canby, February 5, 1925, Barrett Collection.

[52]See Vachel Lindsay, "The Movies," January 13, pp. 302-303; "Back Your Train Up to My Pony," March 10, pp. 166-167; "Venus in Armor," March 28, pp. 380-381; and "Queen of My People," July 7, pp. 280-281, in The New Republic, 1917.

[53]George Scouffas, "Vachel Lindsay: A Study in Retreat and Repudiation," (unpublished Ph. D. dissertation, University of Illinois, 1951), p. 121.

[54]One researcher states that Lindsay lectures on poetry and the movies at the University of Southern California during June and July of 1925. Kuykendall, "The Reading. . . ," p. 52. Another source indicates that Lindsay gave "frequent lectures at the University of Chicago on the Photoplay." John Emerson and Anita Loos, "Photoplay Writing," Photoplay, 24 (June 1918), p. 78.

[55]Vachel Lindsay, "A Letter About My Four Programmes," This flyer was written by Lindsay and apparently privately printed, n. d.

[56]From a typescript of a promotion sheet released by Mrs. Lindsay while acting as manager 1925-29.

[57]From a tract entitled Vachel Lindsay, Troubadour, published by William B. Feakins, Inc., New York. A note in Mrs. Lindsay's hand indicates that the agency assumed management in January 1929.

[58]Vachel Lindsay, "A special Delivery Letter to My Particular Friends" typescript included in a file which Mrs. Lindsay dates 1925-1929, Barrett Collection.

[59]Vachel Lindsay, "The Vitaphone," (unpublished manuscript included in file dated 1925-1929).

[60]Vachel Lindsay, "The Great Douglas Fairbanks," Ladies Home Journal (August 1926), p. 12.

CHAPTER II

Lindsay's America

Towards the end of the last century and during the first decades
of the twentieth, the United States underwent some of the most striking changes in its history. The late nineteenth century witnessed
the rise of industry and a trend toward urbanization. Concurrently,
and as a reaction to this trend, there grew a rather large and powerful
agrarian faction with a very strong political ties. New ideas in education, philosophy, science and psychology were being introduced from
Europe. This was also the period that saw the invention and wide-
spread use of the automobile, the radio, and the motion picture. These
changes were not limited in their effect to the exclusively urban
sections of the country, but affected all parts of it. Lindsay, for
example, was born in a city in which,

> The Gilded Age was commencing, the age of stock gambling,
> and railroad wrecking, of a new kind of swelldom, or
> centralization of money and governmental power. The re-
> public of Jefferson, Jackson, even of Buchanan, was deader
> than the Athenian democracy.[1]

Springfield, Illinois of 1879 was a city which swarmed with politicians
and lawyers intent on expanding the railroads and settling the labor
disturbances common during the period. Lindsay's early years were
spent listening to stories of the trials and tribulations of early
Springfield settlers and recollections of the days when Lincoln and
Douglas roamed about Illinois. That Springfield left a mark on Lindsay
there can be little doubt, for as he later stated: "Everything begins
there and ends there for me."[2]

It is difficult to isolate any specific effects that the changing world of the "guilded age" may have had upon Lindsay's social views, other than the fact that he strenuously objected to some of the changes -specifically industrialization and urbanization. Lindsay was a product of his environment and it was, at least in part, the close tie with his midwestern heritage which led him to view industry and cities as inherently evil. In a sense, his fondness for the midwest and for the small town is exceeded only by his desire to preach their virtues to the entire country. Although he traveled widely and often, he invariably returned to his birthplace, even though there were times during his life when he was scorned by the townspeople of Springfield.

So strong were Lindsay's feelings about the midwest and the small town, that he formulated a plan called "The New Localism" which he believed to be the cultural and moral salvation of the country. It was Lindsay's contention that America could be beautified and thus spiritually improved, only if the small towns would send forth their young people to become artists, poets, architects, actors, singers, etc. These artists would then return to their own individual neighborhoods where they could bring about general cultural improvement among the people and the town itself. Such a plan, Lindsay thought, should be started on the local civic level. Next would come statewide improvement, and finally, unification into a group of uniquely beautiful states. [3] Thus although Lindsay calls his idea The New Localism, he envisioned it as a nationalistic plan which, if properly implemented, knew no boundaries. Without doubt, Lindsay would have been happy with an American patterned after the state of Kansas. He considered Kansas a model to be emulated by the whole nation. Kansas was to Lindsay

the epitome of what our forefathers took for granted. It was free from

large cities and industrialization, was populated by "hardy, devout,

natural" men of the soil, and was a dry state "ruled by the crossroads

church, and the church type of civilization."[4] In short, Lindsay's

idea of what America should be was highly romantic. With considerable

accuracy, Masters says that Lindsay saw America as:

> . . . baseball all through long summer days of white clouds
> and blue skies. He saw it as the prize ring of John L.
> Sullivan, as the white tops of the American circus, the
> only circus of magic in the world. He saw America as movie
> queens, as transcontinental motoring, and as a race of
> youthful dancing sweethearts, crying out the joys of new
> freedoms as they swarmed over a terrene of mountains, plains,
> and forestry; or swam along the Golden coasts of California,
> radiant in the ecstacies of music and passion.[5]

Lindsay's Utopian view of America is strongly indicative of what

Yatron has called a Populist spirit.[6] As Yatron suggests, the word

Populism is at best a rather slippery term which permits no exact de-

finition. The historian, John D. Hicks, speculates that the generic

term, however vague its definition, originated in 1892 at a conference

of Democratic and People's Party leaders who were meeting to discuss

merger plans. One problem which arose was the need for a concise party

name; something other than the cumbersome "People's Party." A Demo-

cratic leader suggested the Latin derived term, populist, which was

immediately adopted.[7] Politically speaking, Populism was largely an

agrarian revolt against landholders and industrialization and was a

unification of the southern and western Farmer's Alliances. Although

Yatron's definition may suffer from deliberate oversimplification and

condensation, it is nevertheless, an adequate illustration of the intellectual background of Populism:

> Populism expressed a way of life that was in opposition to
> the major developments taking place in a rapidly changing
> America. It was a way of life characterized by simplicity,
> hard work, honesty, thrift, and value of the product in
> terms of toil and time rather than in monetary terms.[8]

And in its literary manifestations, we can see how closely the Populist

ideal corresponds with Lindsay's ideal America.

> [It was] mainly reactionary, and by reactionary we mean the
> populists wanted to turn the clock back to a period which
> had ceased to exist a half century before the election of
> 1896. They wanted to return to the river world of Mark
> Twain's Huckleberry Finn, to a boy's world of straw hat,
> bare feet, and fishing pole. On an adult level, this world
> is characterized by small villages and farms, by hard work-
> ing stoic agrarians, who know how to live, love, work, fight--
> and who are thoroughly equalitarian and democratic. Nostalgia
> is, in a word, the essence of the reaction which runs through-
> out literary Populism.[9]

Part and parcel of the Populist belief was the feeling that cities and

technology were not truly representative of America or her art. That

Lindsay is sympathetic with this notion is strongly implied by such

comments as "Art does not travel in a Pullman."[10] However, the personal

credo which Lindsay adopted for his tramping jaunts, best illustrates

his kinship with the Populist spirit:

> These are the rules of the road:
> (1) Keep away from the cities;
> (2) Keep away from the railroads;
> (3) Have nothing to do with money and
>   carry no baggage.[11]

It should be noted that Lindsay's Populist leanings were not unique in

that they found similar expression in the works of other literary figures

such as Edgar Lee Masters, and Carl Sandburg.[12] Art too, had its pro-

ponents of agrarian simplicity in the work of such "regionalists" as

Thomas Hart Benton, John Curry, and Grant Wood.

Like most of Lindsay's ideas, the Populist spirit found its way
into film theory. In the final prophetic chapter of The Art of the
Moving Picture, Lindsay admonishes future film makers to produce films
which:

> Show us the antique United States, with ivy vines upon the
> popular socialist churches, and weatherbeaten images of
> socialist saints in the niches of the doors. Show us the
> battered fountains, the brooding universities, the dusty
> libraries. Show us the houses of administration which
> statues of heroes in front of them and gentle banners
> flowing from their pinnacles. Then paint pictures of the
> oldest trees of the time, and tree-revering ceremonies,
> with unique costumes and a special priesthood.[13]

Lindsay, we have seen, was sympathetic with the populist ideal and
the idea of localism mainly because of his very fundamental objection
to the process of industrialization, the urbanization which must inevitably follow, and the apparent materialism which accompanies such
social changes. It could be argued that such changes are merely
economic ones and thus affect only that aspect of society. Lindsay,
however, believed them to be changes which struck at the very core of
the entire social system and thus would change the fabric of the whole
nation. According to Milton Brown this view was shared by a large
segment of the middle class and dominated its cultural expression.
Perhaps what bothered Lindsay most was the same thing which affected the
art of Charles Burchfield. Brown says: "Burchfield in Salem [Ohio]
experienced the effects of. . . untrammeled industrial expansion at
its worst, for the small towns had not even the cloak of culture which
the concentration of wealth could provide in large cities."[14] It could
be that Lindsay was simply bemoaning the lack of culture in the area
of which he was so fond. However, his concerns appear to go far

beyond his native Springfield and whatever problems may have existed there.

For example, the general pace of American life itself came in for some rather severe criticism. In Lindsay's opinion,

America is literally a land of action, and a land of light. We have reached the point, we have passed the point, of extreme fanaticism in the worship of raw light and raw action . . . . Action and speed and blazing light must alternate with moments of mellowness and rest. Even between each heart beat, there is a split second of absolute rest, which the American spirit would deny. It is the American idea to destroy that split second of rest, which is between every heart beat.[15]

Even the motion picture exhibits the same frenetic atmosphere in its increasing preoccupation with speed. Lindsay compares the development of the film to the man who all his life has detested speed and its inherent dangers but yet buys a Ford car and destroys the "chickens on the road, the dogs and cats and finally his fellow man."[16] Lindsay contends that the motion picture does precisely the same thing to the human mind with the result that:

The whole nervous psychology of the American race has thereby been completely revolutionized. More and more hieroglyphics and more speed, are making one nation of all the tribes and tongues under this government, and really making them one separate tribe. And the rest of the world looks on agast.[17]

Yet, for all his carping about the tempo and the materialism of American life, Lindsay realized that this was the inevitable course of America's development. That he realized this is indicated by his acceptance of the skyscraper, the Ford car and the airplane as genuine American hieroglyphics. The pace, the neon signs, and the glitter of the new American architecture, Lindsay realized, was simply a part of a changing nation. Thus it is not surprising to find him suggesting that film directors

> . . . Make a round of the top ten cent stores in your town,
> and of the soda fountains, or any of the window displays
> of main street, and pause where the glitter is actually
> overwhelming, and say to yourselves: 'This is part of the
> new American hieroglyphics, and no amount of ability of
> old stage tradition can replace it. This is the very
> fabric of American movie life.'[18]

The tone of such a suggestion leaves one with the impression that

Lindsay is perhaps more resigned to such changes than he is happy with

them.

Beyond a basic coldness which he thought it exhibited, Lindsay

believed that one of the major evils of the city was the slums and the

type of existence which the inhabitants were forced to live there. It

was his contention that the confined and drab existence of life in the

slums invariably led to liquor as an escape. The use of alcohol ran

counter to Lindsay's religious upbringing and combating this evil is an

area in which he believed the film to be particularly valuable. His

plan for replacing alcohol with films is outlined in "The Substitutes

for the Saloon," a separate chapter in The Art of the Moving Picture.

Proceeding under the assumption that slums and saloons are mutually de-

pendent, Lindsay argues that the latter can be forced into bankruptcy

and thus obliterated by the addition of movie houses in those slum areas

where saloons are the sole means of relief and socialization. In answer

to the question, "Why do men prefer the photoplay to the drinking place?"

Lindsay replies:

> For no pious reason surely. Now they have fire pouring
> into their eyes instead of into their bellies. Blood is
> drawn from the guts to the brain. Though the picture be
> the veriest mess, the light and movement cause the be-
> holder to do a little reptilian thinking. After a day's

work a street-sweeper enters the place, heavy as King Log.
A ditch-digger goes in sick and surly. It is the state of
the body when many men drink themselves into insensibility.
But here the light is as strong in the eye as whiskey in
the throat. Along with the flare, shadow, and mystery,
they face the existence of people, places and costumes,
utterly novel.[19]

As Lindsay implies, the film offers a release otherwise gained in the

saloon. And, as he is quick to point out, the average slum dweller is

incapable of the imaginative thinking so necessary for a healthy ex-

istence. Thus, he turns either to the saloon or to the film--depending

upon which is most accessible. Exhibiting both his interest in pro-

hibition and his sympathy for the under-privileged, Lindsay states:

Man's dreams are re-arranged and glorified memories. How
could these people reconstruct the torn carpets and tin cans
and waste paper of their lives into mythology? How could
memories of Ladies Entrance squalor be made into Castles in
Granada of Carcassonne? The things they drink to see, and
saw but grotesquely, and paid for terribly, now roll before
them with no after pain or punishment. The mumbled conversation, the sociability for which they leaned over the tables,
they have here in the same manner with far more to talk about.
They come, they go home, men and women together, as casually
and impulsively as the men alone ever entered a drinking place,
but discoursing, now of far off mountains and starcrossed lovers.[20]

Thus we see how the film can serve as a social force; as an instrument

of social good through which the lives of the underpriviledged are made

less mundane; and as an imaginative medium whose peculiar powers enable

it to serve as a substitute for the saloon. And last, but by no means

least in Lindsay's mind, was the fact that the film is ". . . the first

enemy of King Alcohol with real power where the king has deepest hold."[21]

In other words, in an era when prohibition was about to become a nation-

al issue, Lindsay believed that the film was a more powerful force for

eliminating alcohol than all the Chautauqua orators and Anti-Saloon crusaders put together.[22]

In view of Lindsay's discontent with the society in which he found himself, how can we expect him to describe an ideal society? Basic to any answer of this question is the knowledge that Lindsay was not in complete agreement with the political system under which he lived. To a degree, Lindsay, as a result of his Populist sympathies, exhibited socialist tendencies, not in the true Marxist tradition, but only in the sense that he advocated a kind of classless society. Although he may have been discontented with the Democratic system, Lindsay recognized that it was a workable one, for in "The Greatest Movies Now Running," he characterizes it as "a very wasteful method, an overwhelmingly clumsy method, and seemingly the only method."[23] Apparently, part of the problem arises in the use of the word, democracy, itself. As Lindsay says:

> Some people when they speak of democracy mean political and legal democracy, and talk about it so immensely that we forget there is any other sort. Certainly it is the kind most advertised in America. Yet among all this struggling for it since the days of the Civil War, only one has burned himself into my brain, and if there has been only one democrat, is it democracy?[24]

For Lindsay, Democrary was not necessarily a term applied to a political system, but rather it was a state of mind engendered such things as Emerson's essay on Self Reliance; a state of mind engendered by Jeffersonian democracy.[25] This ideal of an intellectual, classless "democracy" was also carried over into Lindsay's pronouncements on film and the arts in general:

> . . . when we speak of democracy in the movies, in antithesis to aristocracy in the movies, let us say, "altgeldism" in the movies and in the arts . . . . No American has ever struggled

to bridge the gap from clean cut Jeffersonian political democracy and the history of American Art. This partly is because we have had no arts fundamentally democratic in their
terms as are our party systems and conventions and pioneer
traditions. As it has been, our snobs have been the custodians
of our arts, and the meanest people on American soil have been
the guardians of beauty, and used beauty as their defense and
their excuse.[26]

Thus, as a name for a social and political system, the word democracy

has more meaning for Lindsay when it is used as a term describing equal-

ity of rights, treatment, and opportunity. It is Lindsay's belief that

the fault of the democratic political system lies in the very fact that

it is not democratic enough; the power of political and cultural choice

is vested in the so-called leaders, and that in itself is cause for

alarm. In Lindsay's opinion, most leaders are not fit custodians of the

arts. Of some of them he says: "We feed up our senators and our

governors until in middle life they are puffy, stupid rhinoceroses,

hippopotamuses, and the like. Not one of them has the originality of an

ordinary elephant or giraffe."[27]

Lindsay's unhappiness with some of the society in which he lived

led him to launch his own personal crusade in an attempt to point out

what he considered to be the ills of society, and to make clear what he

considered to be the ideal society. One of Lindsay's friends said of

him: "He wanted me to disassociate America from the dollar, from the

noisy business rampage, and from all that was unworthy, and instead

identify America with the dreams of her idealists."[28] In order to put

this notion across, Lindsay often resorted to eccentric behavior--in his

tramping, in his poetry recitations, and in his privately published

tracts. What is called eccentricity, however, may be nothing more than

an illustration of Lindsay's idea that a certain degree of flamboyancy

is needed to save America's soul.[29] It would seem that in this flam-
boyance lies the key to what Lindsay sees as the cure for society.

Lindsay insisted that the American dream is a "complete flight to
Utopia,"[30] yet the average American is not capable of making that flight
because of his inhibitions. "The mystic," Lindsay argues "still makes
America squirm. We are not willing to let the moon alternate with the
sun in our fancy. We are not willing to live by moonlight."[31] The
motion picture, however, if allowed the proper freedom, could serve as
the impetus toward that Utopia which is the dream of America. The un-
abashed mysticism of such films as The Thief of Bagdad is, to Lindsay's
way of thinking, an indiction that America is cautious, but yet willing
to start toward its Utopian existence. Lindsay believes that Bagdad as
it exists in The Thief is just magical enough, just enough of an effective fairy tale to serve as a sort of civic example for the United
States. As he puts it:

> There is a princess to win. This princess of national
> happiness is centered in a certain civic prophecy hinted
> at in sky piercers like the Woolworth Tower, or the Medical
> Arts building of Dallas, Texas. The latter in an even more
> brilliant building which few have yet found, but which awaits
> its discoverer and singer. We have achieved epic things in
> this style, and the prophecy of America's future, in the
> very outline of her skyscrapers, is now the newest morning
> the world ever looked upon. We have not achieved the civic
> aspirations nor that American citizenship which these things
> prophesy. Neither have we won that real Queen of Bagdad who
> is dimly prophesied by the Statue of Liberty in New York
> Harbor, by the little shopgirls in O. Henry's stories of
> "Bagdad On the Subway" by Mark Twain's infatuation for Joan
> of Arc.[32]

To summarize, one cannot doubt the nobility of Lindsay's ideas for
the improvement of the society in which he lived, yet it is difficult to
understand his unrealistic view of the inevitable progress of a changing nation. The new Localism, with all its admitted virtues, was

clearly an impracticality; cities, with all their obvious evils, were
a necessity; materialism, be it ever so distasteful, was an inevit-
ability in a nation undergoing an upward economic swing; and democratic
leaders, with all their admitted frailty, were the product of the society
which elected them. It appears that Lindsay too saw the impracticality
of his own preachments and retreated to a more realistic view of what
might be done not necessarily to eliminate these evils, but to make
them less repugnant. This tempered viewpoint becomes most apparent in
his works on film.

Accepting the country for what it was, Lindsay saw very definite
parallels between it and the film. Lindsay thought that American history itself was one giant photoplay which represented "action, intimacy
and splendor of the photoplay sort."[33] Furthermore, he saw a social
parallel between a film such as Monsieur Beaucaire and what he terms a
"Gibson Girl America";[34] he saw a national parallel between the unbroken
rhythm of the film and the natural rhythm of America's high school
youth;[35] and he saw The Covered Wagon as a "thought provoking patriotic
film, that. . . sets us speculating upon every phase of Americanism. in
art and in patriotic thought."[36] We can see then that Lindsay does not
ask film to change, completely, the society in which it exists. Rather,
it should help the people of that society understand themselves, their
society, and their dreams. In terms of our dreams, the task of the film
is to help us become "intimate with the very dragons of our dreams, not
to allow them to be gilt or pasteboard actors, but creatures with whom
we can see some kind of subtly relationships."[37] In terms of our understanding of society, and our heritage,

It is a part of the function of the motion picture to lead
us that way [toward Utopia]. All American history past,
present and to come, in a gigantic movie with a Pilgrim's
progress or hurdle race plot, of sculpture in motion, painting in motion, architecture in motion, fairy splendor, crowd
splendor, religious splendor, patriotic splendor, hieroglyphics in motion, furniture, trappings and inventions in
motion. These things make up American history, our covered
wagon pioneer story on a gigantic scale.[38]

And in terms of understanding ourselves, the film can:

. . . build the American soul broad-based from the foundations.
We can begin with dreams the veriest stone-club warrior can
understand, and as far as an appeal to the eye can do it, lead
him in fancy through every phase of life to the apocalyptic
splendor.[39]

Such is Lindsay's social idealism. And it is this same idealism that

colors his thinking in The Art of the Moving Picture. To all scenario

writers, producers, actors, and "all who are taking the work as a

sacred trust" he says:

Let us resolve that whatever America's tomorrow may be, she
shall have a day that is beautiful and not crass, spiritual,
not material. Let us resolve that she shall dream dreams
deeper than the sea and higher than the clouds of heaven,
that she shall come forth crowned and transfigured with
her statesmen and wizards and saints and sages about her,
with magic behind her and miracle before her.[40]

Hence we see that Lindsay has great visions of a socially beneficial

film art which will help man understand both his country and himself.

But, and this is perhaps the controlling element in Lindsay's entire

philosophy, no society can even approach the Utopia of which he speaks

unless all men of that society have an understanding and an appreciation

of the importance of art. The following chapter will deal with the

function and scope of art in society and the relation of Lindsay's art

theory to his theory of film.

NOTES

[1] Edgar Lee Masters, Vachel Lindsay: A Poet In America (New York: Charles Scribner's Sons, 1935).

[2] Lindsay, Collected Poems, p. 8.

[3] Press clipping, Illinois State Register, December 15, 1910, Barrett Collection. This clipping contains a report of a lecture which Lindsay gave in Springfield.

[4] Vachel Lindsay, Adventures While Preaching the Gospel of Beauty (New York: The Macmillan Company, 1928), pp. 16-19.

[5] Edgar Lee Masters, "Vachel Lindsay and America," Saturday Review of Literature, 12 (August 10, 1935), p. 3.

[6] Michael Yatron, America's Literary Revolt (New York: Philosophical Library, 1959), passim.

[7] John D. Hicks, The Populist Revolt (Minneapolis: University of Minnesota Press, 1931), pp. 238-239.

[8] Yatron, America's Literary Revolt, p. 2.

[9] Ibid., p. 9.

[10] Ibid., p. 84.

[11] Vachel Lindsay, A Handy Guide for Beggars (New York: The Macmillan Co., 1916), p. viii.

[12] Yatron, America's Literary Revolt, passim.

[13] Lindsay, The Art. . ., p. 284-285.

[14] Milton Brown, American Painting from The Armory Show to the Depression (Princeton: Princeton University Press, 1950), p. 177.

[15] Lindsay, "The Greatest. . .," Barrett Collection, pp. 28-29.

[16] Ibid., p. 82.

[17] Ibid.

[18] Ibid., pp. 180-189.

[19] Lindsay, The Art. . ., p. 208.

[20] Ibid., pp. 209-210.

[21] Ibid., p. 214.

[22] Ibid., pp. 210-214.

[23] Lindsay, "The Greatest. . .," Barrett Collection, p. 102.

[24] Ibid., p. 238. The "one who burned himself" into Lindsay's brain was John Peter Altgeld (1847-1902). Elected governer of Illinois in 1892, Altgeld attracted nationwide attention by his actions in the Haymarket riot in Chicago and by his objection to President Cleveland's federal intervention into the Pullman strike. Lindsay's worship of Altgeld can be seen in the poem, The Eagle That is Forgotten.

[25] Ibid.

[26] Ibid., pp. 239-240.

[27] Ibid., p. 114.

[28] Stephen Graham, Tramping with a Poet in the Rockies (New York: D. Appleton and Company, 1928), p. 224.

[29] Ibid., p. 41.

[30] Lindsay, "The Greatest . . .," Barrett Collection, p. 206.

[31] Ibid., p. 138.

[32] Ibid., p. 57.

[33] Ibid., p. 127.

[34] Ibid., p. 179.

[35] Ibid., pp. 232-233.

[36] Ibid., p. 220

[37] Ibid., p.

[38] Ibid., p. 205.

[39] Lindsay, The Art. . ., p. 263.

[40] Ibid., p. 288.

CHAPTER III

Democratic Art

There is little doubt that Lindsay's background in art played an important role in the development of three of his major theoretical constructs, sculpture in motion, painting in motion, and architecture in motion. These constructs, as their names suggest, are firmly grounded upon the graphic and plastic arts. In fact, Lindsay himself says as much: "My own work, such as it has been, has been tied up to my years of lecturing on the history of art, and my theory may be briefly comprehended in the phrase painting in motion."[1] Thus it becomes important to this investigation to examine Lindsay's training in art, and his theory of art.

Vachel Lindsay did not start his career as a poet. Rather, it was his ambition to become an artist, an ambition which he pursued, in terms of formal training, off and on for nearly eight years. After three years of attempting to adjust to the discipline of higher education, and what was supposed to be a pre-medical course, Lindsay ended his formal college education at Hiram College and entered the Chicago Art Institute in 1901. His sojourn in Chicago lasted from 1901 to 1903, and proved to be a lonely and fruitless period of his life. The aspiring young artist quickly found that nearly all of his classmates at the Institute were far better artists than he, or at least fit the pattern of the Institute better. Lindsay accused the Institute of being bare

and stern, and of using "endless old fashioned methods of drawing from
the antique with no word of appreciation, no fellowship with artists,
nothing but stern exercise of hand and eye."[2] Having become disillus-
ioned with himself as an artist, and even more so with the Art Institute
as a training ground, Lindsay persuaded his parents to underwrite a
period of study at the New York School of Art where he would have an
opportunity to study under William Chase and Robert Henri. Thus, in
1903, with the help of two reluctant yet yielding parents, Lindsay entered the New York School and found himself in the company of classmates
such as Rockwell Kent, George Luks and George Bellows. During his stay
in New York, two things seem to have had a lasting influence upon Lindsay: his association with Robert Henri and his continuing study of
art history in the museums of New York. In the words of one biographer
Lindsay's frequent visits to the Metropolitan Museum "gave him a perspective of man's achievement in art from time immemorial to the present;
and seeing what men had done in the past, he surmised the future."[3]
Lindsay's visits were, however, tempered by a critical eye. For, in a
letter to his mother he writes:

> I have a special permit to study the priceless books of
> Utamaro and Hoksai and the rest at the Lenox library,
> and shall try to use it once a week. From the Japanese
> masters I can learn delicacy, spacing, and composition
> and delicacy of color, and beauty of line and of texture--
> everything I want--except the Greek repose and contour--
> and the spiritual majesty of Angelo. One who studies
> Greek too hard draws plaster instead of flesh. . . . One
> who studies Angelo too exclusively runs to distorted
> muscles in the effort for grandeur and exaggerated
> muscles in the effort for strength. The Japanese sins
> are hysteria as I have said, and grotesque. But their
> delicacy when they are best, is incomparable. I hope
> to avoid all these sins and strive for all these virtues.[4]

Precisely how much actual influence Lindsay's visits to museums had on
his practice and theory of art, is difficult to assess because of the
paucity of comment on any of the museums themselves. It is apparent,
that Lindsay did possess a wide knowledge of art history; a knowledge
which manifests itself in his film theory. Whether this knowledge came
from his frequent visits to museums or from his own reading in art
history is difficult to say. The other influence, his relationship
with Chase and Henri, is easier to document through his personal correspondence.

Shortly after his arrival in New York, Lindsay writes, in a re-
assuring tone, "in our school they preach Sargent day and night, so it
is not necessary to apprehend I am learning what will make me unpopular.
Chase, Sargent and Henri paint in essentially the same manner, and are
classed and described in much the same way."[5] Although he equates them
here, later in the same letter, Lindsay expresses his preference for
the teachings of Henri: "He is a greater man than Chase in many re-
spects and insists on force, likeness, and life in the portraits."[6]
Apparently this fondness for the method and the personality of Henri was
a feeling which Lindsay never lost, because nearly a year later his
letters were still filled with his admiration for Henri. In a sense,
this appears to be a case of mutual respect:

> Mr. Henri yesterday met me by accident for the first time
> in a month. He immediately congratulated me on some pen
> and ink sketches exhibited [in] last month's Concour. It
> was my highest honor yet, to have a man like Henri remember
> some grotesque little pen and inks about two months back.
> He is a terribly frank man. It was the character study in
> the pictures he liked. I said, "Mr. Henri I want to get as
> much more drawing into them as possible and retain the loose
> free line." Mr. Henri looked at me as though he wanted to

pitch me into the street. "Haven't I told you drawing isn't
anything? Drawing, why drawing is nothing! Say you are going
to put more and more character into the things, and make them
live. More character--that's what you mean!" I tell the
story since it is the whole of Henri, his Democracy, his posi-
tiveness, his frankness.[7]

It is important to note that growing out of this mutual respect and
admiration, is a trend which later develops into one of the most important facets of Lindsay's training at the New York School of Art.
Here, and elsewhere in Lindsay's correspondence and personal papers, one
can see a growing emphasis on the idea of producing work of art which
exude a sense of life, and even more important, those which are filled
with attempts to capture action. This "action technique" was one of the
key teaching methods of the New York School, and an exercise which
particularly appealed to Lindsay.

In a letter written to his father late in 1903, Lindsay describes
Chase's action technique of life drawing, and applies it to his own
thinking:

I want my people doing something, not in repose--and when you
always draw from a real model that sits still or stands, how
can you make the figure move right when you draw it in imagination? Another nice thing about this class is that there
are four poses an evening. . . and there are two classes a
week, so that will supply me with eight drawings a week--
enough to make a whole group at home and combine them into
some stirring incident.[8]

Beyond his stated fondness for Chase and Henri and their method, Lindsay
found that he was actually doing better work as a result of the New York
School's emphasis on intensity and action drawing. He felt that it
presented a pleasing contrast with the Chicago Art Institute in that in
New York the emphasis was on individuality of style, and speed of ex-
ecution rather than the staid classical exercises of the Chicago school.

As Lindsay puts it, "I have made drawings in half an hour sketch class [which] carried farther, and [were] more accurate than things that took me a week's hard work in Chicago."[9] It appears that Lindsay's individuality coupled with his enthusiasm placed him in good stead in the New York School. There was, however, some slight objection to his tendency toward decorative design, an interest which he never quite lost. Among others, Henri upbraided Lindsay but at the same time recognized his highly personal style. Lindsay gives the following account of an interview with Henri: "When I showed him my Ladies Home Journal cover he said, 'Well, I despise decorative design, but I am forced to admit your work is sincere, you put your own quality into it, it isn't an affection, it is from a genuine love of oriental things, and you are not copying anybody."[10] There is evidence too, that Lindsay constantly sought to reassure his parents regarding his artistic sins. For example, it is not unusual to find him saying such things as, "I shall strive for your ideals of force and democracy in art."[11]

Of prime importance to this investigation is the fact that Lindsay's early training and interest in individuality, spontaneity, and particularly action in art, is something which appears to have carried over into his thinking about the film. One might reasonably expect Lindsay to apply mistakenly the tenets of the graphic arts to film in toto, while completely neglecting the fact that film is a dynamic form. This he did not do, however, and it is conceivable that his early contact with Chase and Henri and their action technique helped him realize that he was dealing with an art form which actually moves rather than one which simply attempts to capture as isolated moment in time. It is, of course, also possible that this interest in spontaneity and movement in art was simply something which Lindsay brought with him to the New York School. Even so, we can say with certainty that the New York School fostered this attitude, rather than stifling it as might have happened had Lindsay stayed at the Chicago Art Institute.

Along with the New York's School's emphasis on action drawing, students were constantly encouraged to practice memory drawing. This was simply a part of the discipline. Lindsay, however, was particularly fond of memory drawing for not only did he find it easier, quicker, and more enjoyable, but it allowed him the freedom of expression which he desired. As he puts it: "I will first study out thoroughly my whole picture--figures and accessories in as hard and fast a way as I can-- and then do the real picture from memory--adding little touches of idealism besides getting in all the facts."[12] Since they are not available for examination, it is difficult to say much about the drawings of Lindsay's art school days, however, it is evident that in later years the drawings which illustrated his books seem to be more influenced by "touches of idealism" than by any genuine attempt at realism. Lindsay's fondness for what he calls "fanciful" and "fantastic accessories" in his drawings was something for which he was criticized throughout his art school days. Even though Chase and Henri are often referred to as proponents of "dark impressionism" their approach to art was still basically representational. And, in this sense Lindsay found it diffi- cult to adjust to the discipline of the School. Henri's insistence up- on individuality of expression led him to recognize Lindsay's work as highly personal and imaginative, thus he was never criticized, but was encouraged to develop along the line which he seemed to be following.

Henri even went as far as to suggest that Lindsay study the work of

Beardsley and the Pre-Raphaelites.[13] It would seem then, that the

major value of the memory drawing activity of the New York School would

be in the realm of fantasy. That is, Lindsay was not adverse to realism,

but was simply of a more fanciful bent, hence memory drawing allowed

him to escape the strictures of representational art and add his own

little bit of "idealism." Eventually, Lindsay turned almost completely

to symbolic expression and the time spent in the New York School may

have nurtured this whole attitude. At any rate, this much is certain:

the training and atmosphere of the New York School of Art stayed with

Lindsay throughout his life, and his film theory, while pictorially

oriented, is nevertheless a theory of moving art. The close relation-

ship which Lindsay found between graphic and plastic arts as we know

them and the film as a type of moving art, clearly can be seen in the

analogy which he uses to describe his own practice of art:

> What I am really doing is making a sculpture-in-motion movie,
> after an elaborate cutting, with rhymned titles. As I put
> down the pencil marks the reel turns and the figures emerge,
> and all thereafter amounts to cutting and putting in the
> titles. . . .
>
> The more intensely and rapidly I work, the more clearly I can
> see the human figure, and I think my normal speed in sketching
> is the speed of the movie reel. As long as I can visualize at
> all, I must learn how to make the pencil go as fast as thought
> . . . . When the pencil does not go as fast as thought, the
> thought or picture is killed like a child falling out of the
> end of the railroad train. Speed will get me pictures I might
> otherwise wait years to make in cold blood. They come and go
> instantly and must be caught by instantaneous photography.[14]

Throughout his life, Lindsay was torn between the practice of poetry

and art. He began his career with the intention of becoming an artist, but drifted into writing even while still a student of art. Yet, Lindsay never lost his devotion to art and the basic belief that his poetry and art should be one in the same. This helps explain Lindsay's desire to furnish, whatever possible, illustrations to accompany his poems. In his mind, the two were inseparable; for every poem there should be at least a mental picture if not a physical one. In a letter written to his mother while still a student at the New York School of Art, Lindsay recognized the basic problem: "I am much more practical and worldly minded during a drawing fit than a writing fit. As a poet I do not fit this world very well. As an artist I can be quite businesslike. That is as it should be for pictures are my business."[15] This is a significant, and early, insight into his own nature and the problem of pursuing both poetry and art. That "pictures were Lindsay's business" is exemplified by his highly rhythmic and imagistic poems which were designed to make his audiences see and feel the ideas presented. At any rate, although Lindsay achieved his fame through his poetry, the graphic and plastic arts and the necessity for them was a consideration which he carried with him throughout life. One of his most comprehensive statements on the position and function of art in society is found in a sermon given at a Springfield church:

> Art is not the most necessary thing in the world. It is never useful, in the American sense. It is often dangerous to the soul like any other pleasure. But the time has come when we must understand it in a religious way. We must know how much and how little it has to do with worship. . . . It is natural to take pleasure in making or seeing beauty. This pleasure has destroyed many nations, because they did not mingle reverence with their pleasure. The necessity for reverence is paramount. . . . Man is a secondary creator. The most savage man makes his pottery splendid with decorative designs. Great architecture, great parks, great rituals testify to man's passion for design. The wisest capitols of the world, the most

> august cathedrals are eye filling glories. But to feast the
> eye on these, as one would on meat or fruit, or flowers, without
> a proper grace before meat without a contrite heart, is to be
> destroyed.[16]

Although the opening of this statement bears a striking similarity to

statements of Oscar Wilde and the art for art's sake movement, we

should not overlook the essential point that Lindsay sees beauty as

serving a useful function. In other words, beauty should never exist

for its own sake, but should instill in the viewer, an awareness of a

higher authority and reverence for the original Creator. In general

terms, then, Lindsay's theory of art is founded upon a belief in an art

of social utility, whereby man's spiritual awareness is increased.

Growing out of this desire for an art which serves a utilitarian

purpose is also a very basic and very strong belief that this purpose is

not served unless art reaches everyone, not just a select minority.

Without qualification, Lindsay believed in a democratic, or if you will,

mass theory of art. Scouffas holds this view, but takes it even further:

He contends that Lindsay had a "democratic theory of communal art based

on the lowest common denominator."[17] It is doubtful that Lindsay's so-

called "lowest common denominator" approach to art was intentional. Since

it was his belief that art was so vital to man's well-being, he des-

perately wanted to reach everyone. As a result of this overwhelming

desire to make some form of art and beauty available to everyone, Lindsay

may have unintentionally catered to the lowest possible taste. Even if

this were the case, one cannot question his motives. Because, it was

Lindsay's basic belief that art becomes truly democratic only when it is

made available to all strata of society. As he puts it, "the arts, like

political parites, are not founded till they have touched the county

chairman, the ward leader, the individual voter."[18] Lindsay's faith
in the democratic ideal, may be a result of the strong influence ex-
erted upon him by his teacher, Henri. Milton Brown has suggested:

> His [Henri's] was essentially the democratic and liberal idea.
> Like Walt Whitman he had faith in man, in the common man, and
> the mass of man, and like Whitman he held aloft the ideal of
> a brotherhood of free individuals. These were the ideals for
> which Henri stood and they were the principles which he tried
> to inculcate in his many students.[19]

Beyond merely reaching the masses, Lindsay is concerned with an art
which actually improves man's lot because it increases his awareness of
the human condition. And, since Lindsay saw the film as the most far-
reaching means of communication yet devised, it is not suprising to find
his clearest statement of this idea in The Art of the Moving Picture:

> We must have Whitmanesque scenarios, based on moods akin to
> that of the poem By Blue Ontario's Shore. The possibility of
> showing the entire American population its own face in the
> Mirror Screen has to come. Whitman brought the idea of
> democracy to our sophisticated literati, but did not persuade
> the democracy itself to read his democratic poems. Sooner or
> later the kinetoscope will do what he could not, bring the
> nobler side of the equality idea to the people who are so
> crassly equal.[20]

Art then, and in this particular case film, must bring to the masses an
awareness of themselves, if it is to fulfill its proper function.

Paralleling Lindsay's idea that successful art is that which is
genuinely democratic in the sense that it reaches the masses, is the
notion that indigenous art is to be valued above all other. This view
can be attributed, at least partially, to Lindsay's feeling that America
as a young nation was in the process of developing her own unique arts.
In a criticism of Lionel Feininger's painting, Lindsay gives us an idea
of what these arts are:

What are the American arts? The skyscrapers, most of them
prohibited by law on European soil, and yet our first
masterpieces; the motion pictures, the flying machine, billboards, and comic strips like Pat Sullivan's "Felix the Cat."
Pictures and enterprises like these we take with such child-
like simplicity. We do not realize that a thousand years
hence we will remember these things then as we remember the
Parthenon now. Amusing new things, produced with such ease
on American soil that we think they are second rate.[21]

Since Lindsay considers these arts to be uniquely American, he further

contends that only the American artist is equipped to express them.

While it may not be the result of any direct influence, this strong

nationalistic spirit was consistent with that of his teacher, Henri.

Brown contends that:

Beginning with Henri, the spirit of nationalism was a fundamental of the realist attitude. They accepted as axiomatic
that an American art should deal realistically with life and
conversely, that a realistic art should concern itself with
America.[22]

So strongly does Lindsay feel that American artists should engage in

"American" art that he urges Feininger, an expatriate, to come home and

"take up American subjects in an American way."[23] Thus we see that Lind-

say desires an art which is American to the core, both in subject matter

and in artist. What Lindsay desires and the standards for comparison

he chooses become contradictory in that he repeatedly uses European art

as examples. For instance, The Art of the Moving Picture abounds in

examples drawn from European art. One explanation for this apparent

contradiction lies in the fact that not only Lindsay, but anyone who

chooses to speak of modern American art, is eventually forced to consider

its highly influential European predecessors. Perhaps an even better ex-

planation is that Lindsay differentiates between the form and the sub-

ject of art. That is, he appears to look to the established classics of art for formal criteria, but then turns to indigenous artists for

subject matter. In a word, it is his feeling that only art of and by

Americans can serve the democratic purpose which he visualizes for art.

In the following, it can be seen that Lindsay admits to the influence

of "non-American" art, yet never quite divorces it from what he sees as

a unique part of our culture:

> Egyptian art is about the only thing not American in art that
> does not leave me a little bit restless and a little bit
> critical. However I may admire the other arts from Japan to
> England, Egypt rests my soul definitely. It is likely through
> a long reconciliation with the rectangular elements in the
> new American arts from the skyscraper steel structure to the
> movie screen, from the advertising billboard to the automobile.24

Although Lindsay pleads for indigenous art and artist, he presents

another of his many interesting contradictions by comparing film with

works of art, most of which are the product of foreign artists. For in-

stance, he suggests that the person viewing a Kandinsky painting ask

himself, "Is that as authoritative to you as the last good movie you

have seen?"25 Moreover, it is Lindsay's contention that modern art is

neglecting formal techniques which are so effectively used by the film.

In a criticism of Feininger's work, Lindsay says:

> All the errors of this mid-European art, which is essentially
> German, are struggles to get away from curves and into
> abstractions which are not the curves of life. Compare this
> one picture [Feininger's The Lady in Mauve] with the movie
> production of John Barrymore in the character of Francois
> Villon. Forget all the actors, and watch in the production
> how even if you blur it from your mind the architecture leaps
> forward and tells the story. Barrymore himself first appears
> as a gargoyle covered with snow overhanging Notre Dame. He
> acts the part as though he were some lean Gothic gargoyle.
> Never is there a loss of grace or the loss of a curve. You
> feel the over-arching sky over the human body, and that whole
> production is full of the mysterious curves of life. But
> this picture represents weariness with those things, and a
> determination to escape into rectangular piano keys in the
> wrong places.26

At least Lindsay is consistent in terms of form in that he suggests that
the paintings of the abstract expressionist school would make ideal back-
grounds for the expressionist film, The Cabinet of Dr. Caligari.
Caligari Lindsay contends, "is an attempt to assemble into one complete
film all the effects which have been achieved all over Europe for ten or
twenty years by men of this school and to put them together into a
consistent story and to put movie action into them."[27] Lindsay is not
at all sympathetic toward expressionism, but it would seem that here, as
in his film theory, he places considerable emphasis upon traditional form,
such as the free flowing curve, and the beauty to be found therein. In
this instance, it happens that Lindsay is not particularly fond of the
angular form used by these artists, hence he completely overlooks the
purpose behind their expressionism. In a sense, these artists were attempting to do precisely what Lindsay suggests is done in his treatment
of the concept of hieroglyphics. But, and this is the critical difference, Expressionism was supposedly intent on externalizing inner emotions
and sensations, whereas Lindsay insists that his hieroglyphic process
was based upon an external manifestation of thought. In the final
analysis, it may be that Lindsay objects to abstraction purely on the
grounds that it neglects, at least in his view, the human element or the
raw material of art. For example, in his discussion of The Thief of
Bagdad, Lindsay describes a scene in which shafts of light acting as
moonbeams, play a major role in the composition. Of this scene he says:

> If the whole story. . . had been told with the same abstract
> intensity of moonbeams, the producers would have achieved that
> thing which seems the ideal of certain modern painters, namely:
> the reduction of all things to pure abstraction of light and

of line. We would have come close to Pater's doctrine, that all
art tends to the conditions of music. It is certainly true of
all other arts, that the nearer they come to pure music the more
they are in peril of destruction. Only for an instant in the
development of a work of art, can it attain to pure music, and
live. From that exalted instant it must move back into the raw
stuff of which it is made with much more definite recognition of
the character of the fabric. It cannot remain abstract long
without complete divorce from human emotions.28

Hence we see Lindsay's concern with the human element of art. It would

seem, however, that the past part of his argument is open to question.

That is, it is tenable that just the reverse is true in terms of ab-

straction and human emotion. In other words, abstraction, because of

its non-representational character, departs from the rational and

logical and depends heavily upon the emotional for its impact--be it

the emotion of the artist or the viewer.

Now that we have examined Lindsay's background in art, and his per-

sonal theories about the position of art in society, the question arises

as to the relationship of these things to his theory of film as an art

form. First, there can be little question that Lindsay views the film

as an art form; young, foolish and stumbling, but still an art. And,

this stumbling youth is one of great potential:

The photoplay art should be literature, and a sacred book,
not a smutty scrawl on an alley fence. It has the possible
dignity of Egyptian hieroglyphics and Egyptian temples, and
the possible splendor of the paintings of Michaelangelo and
Titian, and the possible epic grace of the Russian Dancers.
It should have the apocalyptic gleam that will be the glory
of the future, the prophetic fire already in our most vicious
papers that point toward the future. The Declaration of
Independence, and Lincoln's Gettysburg Address.29

Summarized in this single prophetic statement is Lindsay's view of the

traditional arts, and their relationship to this nascent art form, the

film. We see here, in somewhat metaphoric and perhaps hyperbolic terms, the formalistic carryover from the accepted art classics and the vehement preachment for a truly democratic art. Such a visionary approach to film springs from Lindsay's basic belief that "any complete work of art is a prophecy of a work of art of the future," and that "no creative artist ever looks upon a work as complete."[30] The film then, as a work of art, is not a finite product, but continues to build upon itself. It builds, and in a sense is superior to the traditional arts, because it is capable of producing "pictures beyond the skill of any delineator in the old mediums."[31] Finally, the recources of visualization which enable film to surpass the traditional arts in communicative power, make it a great symbolizing force capable of producing a "higher form of picture writing" which ultimately will become a "higher form of vision-seeing."[32]

To this point, we have seen that Lindsay looks upon art as an absolutely essential element of a healthy democratic society. Yet, perhaps the most important function of art has not been discussed in any detail--that is Lindsay's belief that art is a means of spiritual salvation. The following chapter will deal with Lindsay's personal religious beliefs and his contention that if art is an art of beauty, it can reveal the presence of God, thus serving the highest possible social function.

NOTES

[1] Lindsay, Why I Think . . ., Barrett Collection, p. 25.

[2] Letter to Mrs. Vachel Lindsay, April 2, 1904, Barrett Collection.

[3] Albert Edmund Trombly, Vachel Lindsay, Adventurer (Columbia, Missouri: Lucas Brothers, 1929), p. 37.

[4] Letter to Mrs. Vachel Lindsay, January 31, 1904, Barrett Collection.

[5] Letter to Dr. and Mrs. Vachel Lindsay, November 10, 1903, Barrett Collection.

[6] Ibid.

[7] Letter to Mrs. Vachel Lindsay, April 2, 1904, Barrett Collection.

[8] Letter to Dr. Vachel Lindsay, November 3, 1903, Barrett Collection.

[9] Letter to Dr. and Mrs. Vachel Lindsay, November 10, 1903, Barrett Collection.

[10] Letter to Mrs. Vachel Lindsay, April 2, 1904, Barrett Collection.

[11] Letter to Dr. and Mrs. Vachel Lindsay, November 10, 1903, Barrett Collection.

[12] Letter to Dr. Vachel Lindsay, November 14, 1903, Barrett Collection.

[13] From a personal diary, January 3, 1905, Barrett Collection.

[14] "Charter Copy," unpublished manuscript, n.d., Barrett Collection.

[15] Letter to Mrs. Vachel Lindsay, March 17, 1904, Barrett Collection.

[16] Press clipping which reported the sermon as follows: "The necessity of Reverence: An able discourse by Nicholas Vachel Lindsay, delivered to the congregation of the First Christian Church at regular Sunday Morning services yesterday," n.d., Barrett Collection.

[17]Scouffas, "A Study in Retreat. . . ," p. 52.

[18]Lindsay, The Art. . . ," p. 185.

[19]Brown, American Painting. . . , p. 11.

[20]Lindsay, The Art . . . , pp. 65-66.

[21]Vachel Lindsay, "Blue Four Review," n.d., Barrett Collection, p. 5. This review, which covers the painting of Lionel Feininger, Alexei von Jawlensky, Wassily Kandinsky, and Paul Klee, is apparently Lindsay's reaction to a traveling exhibit entitled European Modernists. Although the manuscript is undaded, Lindsay's papers contain a gallery program dated 1927. Hence it is likely that Lindsay wrote the review in Spokane, Washington.

[22]Brown, American Painting . . . , p. 137.

[23]Lindsay, "Blue Four. . . ," p. 1.

[24]From a personal notebook, February 12, 1926, Barrett Collection.

[25]Lindsay, "Blue Four. . . ," p. 16.

[26]Ibid., pp. 1-2.

[27]Ibid., p. 9.

[28]Lindsay, The Greatest. . . , Barrett Collection, pp. 83-84.

[29]Lindsay, "Special Delivery Letter. . . ," Barrett Collection.

[30]Lindsay, "The Greatest. . . ," Barrett Collection, p. 56.

[31]Lindsay, The Art. . . , p. 283.

[32]Ibid., p. 271.

CHAPTER IV

Religion and Beauty

Of vital importance to an understanding of Lindsay's film theory, and for that matter, his entire aesthetic, is an appreciation of his general religious beliefs. In Lindsay's lexicon, art and religion are nearly synonymous, and one can be understood only in light of the other. This chapter will be devoted to an examination of the relationship between art and religion in an attempt to demonstrate how this kinship manifests itself in Lindsay's film theory.

Lindsay was born into a family that traced its religious ties almost to the beginning of "The Disciples of Christ," a sect based upon the teachings of Alexander Campbell.[1] His parents were zealous "Campbellites" and apparently instilled in young Lindsay, a religious fervor which stayed with him throughout his life. Furthermore, Lindsay was born and raised in a community permeated with the Campbellite spirit. The Disciples had established a church in Springfield in 1820, just one year after the first Campbellite church in the state of Illinois.[2]

Although Lindsay was a nominal member of the Disciples of Christ, he did depart from the literalist, fundamentalist tradition of Campbellite theology. For example, we can see his radical thinking in such statements as "It is my entirely personal speculation. . . that scripture is not so much inspired as it is curiously and miraculously inspiring."[3] Of course, such a statement strikes at the very core of Campbellite theology because it questions the literal interpretation of scripture.

Late in life Lindsay became disenchanted with his fellow Disciples.

He accused them of having mistrusted him "from start to finish" and of

"never [taking] an hour to go straight through all my books and assemble

the evidence that I am as much interested in the ups and downs of "The

Brotherhood" as the editors of The Evangelist, The Standard, The Christ-

ian, or The Christian Century."[4] Nevertheless, regardless of what the

Brotherhood may have thought of Lindsay and his work, Lindsay himself

was fully confident of his ties with the faith. As he puts it:

> I cannot pretend to be religious, but I know I am an utterly
> incurable follower of the high campanion of the intellec-
> tual frontier "primitive" life, Alexander Campbell. I am
> just a member of his tribe as a Choctaw is a member of the
> Choctaw tribe.[5]

In brief then, the Campbellite faith is one to which Lindsay claimed

allegiance throughout his life, even in view of his suspicion of his

fellow Disciples and his personal departure from the basic dogma. These

apparent departures from Campbellite theology may be, in reality, only

a matter of Lindsay placing greater emphasis upon individuality.

Llewelyn Jones suggests a similar idea in his analysis of Lindsay's

religion:

> His sect did not mean to him a rallying place for whatever
> religious doctrines the original Campbellites may have preached.
> It meant to him a personal fellowship with those preachers.
> For Lindsay, the essence of religion was this personal con-
> tinuity: something you have inherited by tradition and even
> by blood. . . he preached that not only is your personal
> religion your home town religion but your only real culture
> is your home town culture.[6]

Until the time he left Hiram College, a Disciples supported in-

stitution, Lindsay apparently was not motivated to investigate the teach-

ings of other faiths. However, once he left the strong Campbellite influence of his family, and the religious atmosphere of college, he

cultivated an interest in other faiths. During his art students days

in New York, he developed an interest in Catholicism. He not only

studies the faith, but also attended mass. In a letter which no doubt

shook his zealous Campbellite parents to the core, Lindsay says:

> I attended the church of the Paulist Fathers, the most liberal
> Catholics of America I have been told. . . . He [the priest]
> preached a sermon that was so high minded and spiritual it
> could have suited a Kentucky Campbellite without suspicion, or
> a Salvation Army Barracks. . . I was very glad to understand
> the church as it sees itself, and hope to go some more. They
> use the Gregorian chant, the oldest and finest church music
> in the world. It, is said to be one of the musical treats of
> New York.[7]

Although Lindsay appears fascinated with Catholicism, he registers sur-

prise that such a "high minded" sermon could come from a Catholic. On

the other hand, it could be that such a remark was inserted merely to

allay any fears his parents may have had about his serious interest in

the faith. That Lindsay remained skeptical is evidenced by a later

letter in which he tells his parents that "there is lots more good and

lots more bad in the church than I dreamed."[8] From all indications,

Lindsay's interest in Catholicism centered around the externals of the

faith, the ornateness of the ritual, and the church architecture itself,

rather than Catholic theology.

In addition to his interest in Catholicism, Lindsay is known to

have dome some reading and investigation of Buddism, Confucianism, and

Swedenborgianism.[9] It is from Swedenborgianism that Lindsay appears to

have derived some of his ideas about art, particularly in the realm of

symbolism; yet Lindsay insists that he was never a "literal Sweden-

borgian."[10]

The teachings of Emanuel Swedenborg,[11] the Swedish mystic, seem particularly well suited to both the personality of Lindsay, and to the

purpose he assigned to art. Heffernan contends:

> Two essential qualities in the nature of Lindsay inevitably
> drew him to Swedenborg--his mysticism and his penchant for
> making everything stand externally for some inner nature.
> The former accounts for his vision seeing and the latter for
> his symbols and hieroglyphics, both of which, though not
> necessarily derived from Swedenborg, provide significant
> points of contact with him.[12]

Swedenborg's teachings, based in large part upon what he called the

"doctrine of correspondences," hold that all outward and visible things

have some sort of inward and spiritual cause. He suggested that there is

a precise correspondence between thought and expression, regardless of

what form that expression may take--speech, writing, art, etc. In terms

of scriptural interpretation, Swedenborg saw various elements of the

physical world as symbolic of the spiritual order. For instance, the

scriptural use of stone stands for truth and knowledge; water likewise

stands for truth; love and faith are presented by the sun and the moon;

and the stars serve as guides to spiritual truth when other spiritual

lights are obscured. Furthermore, such famous Biblical stories as the

flood and the Tower of Babel are, in Swedenborg's system, simply parables

which metaphorically illustrate, respectively, the flood of evils and

falsities of the modern church, and man's efforts to circumvent God's

established order of life and climb to heaven via another route. If

Lindsay adhered to such doctrines, and we have no way of knowing if he

did or not, it would have constituted a severe departure for him from

the strict literalist tradition of Campbellite theology.

Another aspect of Swedenborg's system important to Lindsay is

Swedenborg's notion that what a man's hands produce is an illustration of his inner character. As one interpreter of Swedenborg sees this doctrine,

> No history is so true as that which is written in the art of a people. Architecture is an embodiment of national life, and even the fashioning of every day objects reveals something of the character and ideals of a community. In fact, every act of man is the outcome and expression of his soul, and corresponds to the latter in a manner more or less perfect.[13]

This one tenet of Swedenborgianism contains the real essence of Lindsay's feeling about art and film as an art. That is, art is the genuine expression of both the man and his milieu. Likewise, it is Lindsay's contention that film, when it fulfills its true purpose, is an expression of the most noble and worthy principles of America.

It is difficult, if not impossible, to be sure whether Swedenborg's theories had any direct influence upon Lindsay and his concept of hieroglyphics. In "The Greatest Movies Now Running," for example, Lindsay refers to Swedenborg as "the great photoplay director" whose mysticism is "so close to the hieroglyphics and psychology of the motion picture."[14] There is also an interesting parallel between Swedenborg's "correspondences" and Lindsay's concept of film hieroglyphics. For example, Swedenborg interpreted Adam and Eve as representatives of the entire race or human nature. Adam represented man's intellectual nature and Eve his emotional nature. These two "symbolic" characters present a striking similarity to Lindsay's theory that the film tends to produce in its crowd genre, a single hieroglyphic figure who is the representative of the entire ethnic group from which he comes. In addition, Lindsay like Swedenborg, is prone to isolate material objects as symbolic of ideas. For example, he contends that in the film, the sea is representative of the "sea of humanity." Extending this similarity, we find that in the systems of both Swedenborg and Lindsay symbols are based upon pre-existing external manifestations. Consequently, the person who would express himself through symbols, need not _invent_ them. He need only hunt for an appropriate physical reality and establish the relationship between it and the idea to be conveyed.

To summarize with accuracy Lindsay's connection with various traditional religious faiths is to admit his interdenominationalism. His interest in the Disciples of Christ, Catholicism, Buddism, Confucianism, and Swedenborgianism is a rather strong indication that he longed for and believed in a universal church.[15] Evidence of any direct influence of religion upon his film theory is much more difficult to document; however, there are some apparent similarities between Swedenborg's "correspondences" and Lindsay's hieroglyphic method.

Of more importance than the effect of any one specific religious belief on Lindsay's film theory, is an understanding of the role which religion plays in the formulation of his fundamental philosophy. In large part Lindsay's philosophy, or his interest in the human condition, is governed by his boundless faith in art. In fact, it is virtually impossible to determine where Lindsay's art theories end and his religious beliefs begin, for the two are mutually dependent in his aesthetic. The remainder of this chapter will be given to an examination of this relationship.

In a 1907 notebook, Lindsay began to outline a mission for himself which was to be a part of his basic philosophy and a part of the salvation which he was to preach in his poetry, in his art, and in his film theory. In short, the idea is this: "Beauty is the manifestation

of God--let all men bow down before it."[16] Lindsay felt that helping

men to understand this relationship between beauty and God, was a part

of his own personal mission.

To Lindsay art was one thing and beauty quite another, and the

mere fact that a person cultivates a love of art does not mean that he

will therefore be capable of recognizing beauty. He felt that there was

ample opportunity to learn the love of art, but that man was in need of

someone or something to instill in him, a genuine "beauty consciousness";

a consciousness which ultimately would lead to the realization that all

beauty is but an external manifestation of God. All men, Lindsay felt,

are inherently capable of responding to beauty; of this there can be no

doubt. The problem is, however, that man must be made to understand

that the recognition of beauty is a moment of revelation. "Men," Lindsay

wrote, "must fervently believe, as a fanatical faith, not as a sentiment

or dream, but as the first canon of their orthodoxy, that the beauty of

the world is the progressive revelation of God."[17] In a statement of

his own faith, and the faith that he felt he must spread throughout the

land, Lindsay proclaimed:

> Beauty is the only salvation of my faith--the sense of beauty
> is the only salvation of the faith of mankind in the presence
> of science. These fervors must be kindled, else man will lose
> his soul. I would like to pour enough attar of roses in the
> ocean to take the salt away--I would like to pour enough beauty
> sense into the American people to change them forever and ever.
> I must list the propositions I am able to maintain. Beauty is
> the salvation of my Faith, and Faith in man's sense of Beauty
> is to me faith in God.[18]

Hence Lindsay's religion, in part, is an aesthetic in which there was a

very close relationship among art, beauty, and God. We see then, that in Lindsay's hierarchy the ideal way to God is by using the capabilities inherent to all men. That is, man can be taught the love of art, and all men respond to the beauty therein, therefore all that remains is for man to realize that this beauty is the manifestation of God. And, it is the last of this tripartite religious aesthetic--showing man the presence of God in beauty--which Lindsay sees as his personal mission.

It should be noted, that although Lindsay added a religious dimension to the function of beauty, his idea of beauty as the proper province of art is consistent with nineteenth and early twentieth century realist philosophy. John I. H. Baur points out that the realist philosophy of the nineteenth century was one which insisted that the duty of the artist is to "reveal an objective and pre-existing beauty in nature rather than create a new beauty in terms of art."[19] Nature was looked upon as the source of beauty, and it was the artist's responsibility to become sensitive to the beauties of the visual world in order that he might "discover and mirror them for the delight of less perceptive eyes."[20] Lindsay believed that his job was the same as these nineteenth century realists except for the added responsibility of making clear to the "less perceptive eyes." that this beauty is actually the manifestation of God. Yet, even in this, Lindsay's ideas were not entirely revolutionary. Asher Durand, some fifty years earlier, had held that the beauties of nature had in them the force of religious revelation.[21] In the final analysis then, Lindsay differs markedly from the traditional realist philosophy only in that he proposes a different formal method for exposing this beauty--the film.

What grew out of these ideas which were first set down by Lindsay in 1907 was a privately printed tract entitled The Gospel of Beauty.

In it he espoused the basic notion of salvation through beauty, but in

a somewhat more prescriptive fashion than he had in his notes of 1907.

In the summer of 1912, Lindsay took this tract and set out from Spring-

field on one of his walking trips. This time he headed for Califor-

nia.[22] This accounts for the first sentence of the "prologue" in which

Lindsay says:

> I. Prologue. I come to you penniless and afoot, to bring a
> message. I am starting a new religious idea. The idea does
> not say "no" to any creed that you have heard. After this,
> let the denomination to which you now belong be called in
> your heart "The Church of Beauty" or "The Church of the Open
> Sky." The Church of Beauty has two sides: The love of
> beauty and the love of God.[23]

Essentially, what Lindsay has to say in this proclamation is the same

as the ideas which we have just examined. The art, beauty, God hierarchy

remains but the Gospel of Beauty is more specific in its suggestions as

to how to attain the pinnacle. The ideas in this tract are of suffi-

cient import for the purposes of this paper, to justify quoting in their

entirety.

> II. The New Localism. The things most worthwhile are one's own
> hearth and neighborhood. We should make our own home and
> neighborhood the most democratic, the most beautiful and the
> holiest in the world. The children now growing up should become
> devout gardeners, or architects, or part architects, or teachers
> of dancing in the Greek spirit, or musicians, or novelists, or
> poets, or story writers, or craftsmen, or wood carvers, or
> dramatists, or actors, or singers. They should find their
> talent and nurse it industriously. They should believe in
> every possible application to art theory of the thoughts of the
> Declaration of Independence and Lincoln's Gettysburg Address.
> They should, if led by the spirit, wander over the whole nation
> in search of the secret of democratic beauty with their hearts
> at the same time filled to overflowing with the righteousness
> of God. Then they should come back to their hearth and neighbor-
> hood and gather a little circle of their own sort of workers
> about them and strive to make the neighborhood and home more
> beautiful and democratic and holy with their special art. They
> should labor in their little circle expecting neither reward
> nor honors. In their darkest hours they should be made strong

by the vision of a completely beautiful neighborhood and the
passion for a completely democratic art. Their reason for
living should be that joy in beauty which no wounds can take
away, and that joy in the love of God which no crucifixion
can end.24

In addition to giving more specific suggestions as to how his

idea of salvation through beauty may be promulgated, Lindsay inserts the

familiar dimension of democratic art. It will be remembered from the

discussion of art, that Lindsay insists upon a truly democratic art.

Again, we find this democratic idea in The Gospel of Beauty, this time

in connection with a plan called "The New Localism." Localism as a

part of the overall Gospel, was a plan to which Lindsay gave a great

deal of thought and expression throughout his Life. He thought that

the gospel as a whole would best be implemented by starting on the local

level with a beautification of small town America. This almost bound-

less faith in small towns as a collection of potential cultural meccas,

is one which springs not only from a fondness for the midwest from

which he came, but also is the result of a reaction against the burgeon-

ing industrialization and urbanization which was taking place at the

time. Lindsay's ideas about the social ills of the time will be dis-

cussed in more detail in the chapter which follows. But for now, suffice

it to say that the idea of localism was, in part, a means whereby Lind-

say believed that he could combat the moral evil of the large city.

How then does the literal religious gospel of beauty manifest itself

in his film theory? Generally speaking, it is perhaps the most per-

vasive aspect of Lindsay's theory. Sculpture, painting, and architec-

ture in motion are firmly grounded upon a foundation of formal con-

siderations, the ultimate purpose of which is to produce the most

pleasing and meaningful visual effects possible. The resultant beauty
is, of course, only a means to the attainment of a higher end--an
awareness of the spiritual source. It should be added, however, that
beauty need not result from formal considerations alone, but can come
from nearly any facet of the film. For instance, Lindsay contends that
the star system contributes to the beauty of the film. Speaking of
Mary Pickford, he says: "The People are hungry for this fine and
spiritual thing that Botticelli painted in the faces of his muses and
heavenly creatures. Because the mob catch the very glimpse of it in
Mary's face, they follow her night after night in the films."[25] In this
statement we have a characteristic example of Lindsay's contention that
every man is capable of responding to beauty. It is apparent that he
personally looks to the film to purvey a kind of beauty, which in some
cases is highly subjective, and cannot be relied upon to appeal to everyone. At any rate, such examples add credence to Lindsay's argument that
"beauty is not directly pious, but does more civilizing in its proper
hour than many sermons or laws."

Although Lindsay was a nominal member of The Disciples of Christ,
his personal practice of that faith did not concern itself with the
particulars of Campbellite dogma. His was not a faith aimed at the
salvation of his own soul, so much as it was a highly developed evangelistic faith which led him to worry about the basic humanistic problem
of what he could do to improve man's lot. To Lindsay, who possessed a
keen spirit of interdenominationalism, whatever faith a man claimed was
his own business. Lindsay did contend, however, that it was his own
personal task to make every man fully aware of the source of his faith,

and to show him the means whereby that faith might be renewed. This could be done only by convincing man that all beauty is the progressive revelation of God. This was Lindsay's religious mission; a mission to be fulfilled not on the basis of pure religious preachments alone, but one built upon what Lindsay considered to be the close relationship between art and religion. If man can be taught to appreciate the source of beauty, then by means of an art which is beauty-centered, man's spiritual condition can be improved. Film then, because it is an art of beauty, and because it is capable of reaching a far greater audience than the traditional arts, becomes, at once, an artistic and religious instrument whereby Lindsay may preach his literal Gospel of Beauty.

This section of the study has been concerned with an analysis of some of the factors which appear to have influenced Lindsay's thinking about the function and scope of film in society. We have seen that he was both discontented with, and resigned to the society in which he lived, but that film, like all the arts, has the potential of helping man improve and adjust to society. Finally, it was noted that all art, film included, if it is truly beautiful, can serve as the revelation of God thus fulfilling the supreme social function. The conclusion is obvious. Lindsay sees the film as a socially beneficial art, not merely as means of frivolous escapism. As yet we have not examined the specifics of the way in which film is, or may become, a beneficial art of beauty. Therefore, the next section of the study will be concerned with the "hows" of film structure, or more specifically, an analysis of Lindsay's structural theories.

NOTES

[1]The Disciples of Christ, known also as the "Chrisitan Church" or "Church of Christ," was started by Thomas Campbell a member of the Seceder branch of the Presbyterian church in northern Ireland. Campbell, who was imbued with an intense feeling against the sectarianism of his day, found it necessary to withdraw from Presbyterian jurisdiction and continue his fight for Christian unity. Briefly, Campbell's mission was the union of all Christians, upon the basis of the divine order of faith and practice as revealed by the New Testament. From 1812 to 1850 the faith was strengthened and grew under the leadership of its founder's son, Alexander Campbell. Young Campbell applied himself to a study of the New Testament in an effort to discover a divine justification for the union of all faiths. To this day, disciples still consider as their primary purpose, the restoration of unity among Christians, and they seek to accomplish this by the restoration of New Testament Christianity in faith and practice. In terms of specific doctrines, the Disciples adhere to: (1) congregational autonomy, (2) the use of biblical names to describe the church, (3) Baptism of the penitent by immersion, (4) confession of faith in Christ as the son of God, and (5) weekly communion. For a detailed description of Campbellite theology see Royal Humbert (ed.), A Compend of Alexander Campbell's Theology (St. Louis: Bethany Press, 1961).

[2]Winfred Earnest Garrison and Alfred T. DeGroot, The Disciples of Christ: A History (St. Louis: Christian Board of Publication, 1948), p. 221.

[3]Lindsay, The Art. . . , p. 287.

[4]Letter to Burris A. Jenkins, July 12, 1927, Cockerell Collection. These publications were the leading Disciples Journals of the period.

[5]Letter to Marguerite Wilkinson, July 4, 1927, Cockerell Collection.

[6]Llewellyn Jones, "Vachel Lindsay: American Poet," Christian Century, 48 (December 23, 1931), p. 619.

[7]Letter to Mrs. Vachel Lindsay, February 19, 1904, Barrett Collection.

[8]Letter to Mrs. Vachel Lindsay, March 16, 1904, Barrett Collection.

[9]This writer has been unable to isolate any direct influence of Buddha or Confucius on Lindsay's thinking about the film. Masters says that Lindsay had great admiration for both Confucius and Buddha, mainly

because of their ascetism and mysticism. Furthermore, Masters credits Lindsay with having said that Buddha was "the supreme personality of history." Edgar Lee Masters, Vachel Lindsay. . . , p. 297.

[10]Lindsay, Collected Poems, p. xxxvi.

[11]Emanuel Swedenborg (1688-1772), son of a theology professor, was born in Stockholm. Initially, his fame came from his far-reaching experiments in the fields of geology and physiology. However, in 1745, Swedenborg received a direct revelation from God, which led him to resign his position as the federal mining expert in order that he might devote his full energies to scriptural study. His studies of the scriptures resulted in voluminous elaboration of his idea that the essence of God is love, that nature and spirit are distinct, and that man's function is to remake himself in the image of God. It was Swedenborg's contention that in scripture, God reveals himself through the natural, spiritual, and celestial senses. All of these beliefs were the result of what Swedenborg felt was his divine commission. For a detailed account of Swedenborg's life and teachings, see Signe Toksvig, Emanuel Swedenborg: Scientist and Mystic (New Haven: Yale University Press, 1948).

[12]Miriam Margaret Heffernan, "The Ideas and Methods of Vachel Lindsay" (unpublished Ph.D. dissertation, New York University, 1948), p. 45.

[13]George Trobridge, Swedenborg: Life and Teaching (New York: Swedenborg Foundation, 1944), p. 152.

[14]Lindsay, "The Greatest. . .," Barrett Collection, p. 138.

[15]Heffernan, "The Ideas. . . ," p. 49.

[16]From a personal notebook, July 20, 1907, Barrett Collection.

[17]Ibid.

[18]Ibid.

[19]John I. H. Baur, Revolution and Tradition in Modern American Art (Cambridge: Harvard University Press, 1951), p. 12.

[20]Ibid.

[21]Ibid.

[22]Lindsay aptly called "the vagabond poet" started the first of his extended tramps across the country in 1906. This trip started in Flordia and ended in Kentucky. In 1908, with New York City as a base, he walked through New Jersey and Pennsylvania. Lindsay's 1912 expedition started in Springfield, with Los Angeles as the final destination. He walked as far as Las Vegas, where he wired home for train fare for the remainder of the trip. In 1921, along with Steven Graham, the English poet, Lindsay hiked through Glacier National Park. For an account of the last trip, see Steven Graham, Tramping. . . ., Lindsay's tramping tours apparently stimulated his creative spirit, for during these periods he wrote some of his poetry and kept voluminous diaries which detailed his reflections on the people and the country. For a detailed chronicle of Lindsay's trips, see, Masters, Vachel Lindsay. . . .

[23]Vachel Lindsay, The Gospel of Beauty, Broadside privately published, 1912.

[24]Ibid.

[25]Lindsay, The Art. . . ., p. 28.

[26]Ibid., p. 251.

PART II

THE THEORETICAL CONSTRUCTS

CHAPTER V

Sculpture in Motion

In his opening chapter entitled "The Point of View" Lindsay outlines the method and purpose of the entire book. Here it is made
clear that The Art of the Moving Picture is a book not for a selective
audience of critics, theorists, or movie makers, but rather one which
is primarily for those who make up the audience. It therefore might
also be entitled "How to Classify and Judge the Current Films."[1] True
to his own suggestion, Lindsay classifies. He does so initially by
maintaining that there are three genres of photoplays with which he
will deal: Action, Intimacy, and Splendor. It is the first of these,
action and its corollary, sculpture in motion, which this chapter will
treat. Although Lindsay's treatment of the action picture is not
lengthy, it is far less circuitous than his discussion of the other
two categories, Intimacy and Splendor.

Lindsay speaks first of the action picture as that genre of
photoplay in which the "outpouring of physical force of high speed is
the main source of the drama."[2] Refining and enlarging this notion
somewhat, he later describes the action picture as having "its photographic basis or fundamental metaphor in the long chase down the high-
way."[3] This illustration is extended to include any and all photoplays
whose essential character is one of chase or action rather than those
films which revolve, primarily, around quite intellectual and emotional
interplay between characters. Genuine character development is

sacrificed for a sort of stereotypic figure who does little more than
lend himself to a swiftly moving action-filled plot. As Lindsay puts
it:

> In the action picture there is no adequate means for the
> development of any full grown personal passion. The dis-
> tinguished character study that makes genuine, the personal
> emotions in the legitimate drama, has no chance. People
> are but types, swiftly moved chessmen.[4]

He contends that the legitimate stage concerns itself with the slow and
deliberate creation of a dramatic intensity which arises from the pity,
revenge, joy, and gratification resulting from the interplay of
characters within the drama. The film, on the other hand, the action
picture included, often _appears_ to deal with such things but, in fact,
uses substitutes such as "the excitement of speed-mania stretched on the
framework of an obvious plot."[5] In addition, the action picture deals
in a sort of "generalized pantomime" as opposed to the more highly in-
dividualized expression of the stereotyped figure.[6] In short then, the
action picture is characterized by action and impersonality, by a certain fabricated dramatic intensity. The "chased" or the object of the
conflict becomes as important, or more important than the persons of the
drama. It is a genre which satisfies the appetite of both the medium
and its audience for movement, speed, and chase.

At this point, two pertinent questions arise regarding the action
picture. First, what hope is there for a genre which Lindsay deprecates,
or at least sees as having some very serious dramatic and intellectual
limitations? Lindsay's position is at least partially explained by his
desire to attach to all of his "classifications" some sort of artistic
justification from the area with which he is most familiar, the graphic

and plastic arts. Hence, it is this type of picture, the action pic-

ture, which Lindsay describes as sculpture in motion. The second ques-

tion is, of course, why sculpture in motion? A partial answer might be

found in his unpublished work, "The Greatest Movies Now Running":

> Action pictures bring the individual actors, the hero, the
> heroine, the villian, very close to the screen. He almost
> leans out of it upon the audience, as though the head and
> shoulders of a giant were leaning out of a great window and
> we see the body of hero and heroine magnified like the
> Colossus of Rhodes, and more and more of these actors are
> chosen for their great beauty and symmetry, and so we have
> sculpture in motion, especially demanded in the hurdle race
> plot that marches down the road. [sic]7

As a specific instance of sculpture in motion, Lindsay cites The Thief

of Bagdad, a 1924 production starring Douglas Fairbanks. In this par-

ticular film he sees a palace guard as not only a form of sculpture,

but as a good filmic representation of a particular medium; namely bronze:

> So near to the camera is he, so thoroughly does he fill the
> eye, that his gleaming and magnificent bronze body, against
> a purely abstract background is literally bronze sculpture.
> It is surely sculpture in motion, carrying into the fourth
> dimension, whatever element it may be that sculpture has
> brought into the world of photoplay art.8

Furthermore, bronze possess certain aesthetic resources that lend them-

selves to the picturization demanded by the action photoplay's propensity

for the exhibition of the anatomical structure of both man and beast.

If the film maker patterns his photography after the bronze statue, then

the film, like bronze, will tend to emphasize the elasticity and pan-

therlike quality of the figure.9 Just as bronze is particularly adapted

to the visual presentation of the figure, so do particular figures lend

themselves to the bronze-like photography. The photoplay of the Amer-

ican Indian should, for instance, "be planned as bronze in action."10

Again speaking of The Thief of Bagdad, and again emphasizing the sculpturesque quality of the figure, Lindsay seems to be influenced not only
by the line and texture of the figure, but also by image size.

> See how the sentinels are combatants close to the camera and
> are gigantic bronzed figures much larger than life and carved
> as by a living chisel. Forget how large they are until you
> compare them with the face of the clock by the side of the
> stage. Or see how the hand of prince or princess can be big
> as the whole screen without being in any way inelegant or
> silly, but seeming as delicate a hand as the hand of Tom
> Thumb's wife.[11]

Interestingly enough, Lindsay feels that it is the film's ability to
convey this sense of plasticity, which distinguishes it from other art
forms. The theatre, for instance, does not, as he puts it, "appeal to
the plastic sense in this way." Rather,

> . . . the little far away people on the old fashioned speaking
> stage. . . are by comparison, mere bits of pasteboard with
> sweet voices, while, on the other hand, the photoplay fore-
> ground is full of dumb giants. The bodies of these giants are
> in high sculptural relief.[12]

At this point, one is tempted to conclude that Lindsay is interested only in a type of film, or photography if you will, which is pictorially pleasing, yet static. This, of course, would be a negation of
one of the capabilities of the film. And, such is not the case with
Lindsay. While it is true that considerable emphasis is placed on the
purely linear and textural aspect of sculpture, he does not neglect the
important aspect of movement. Lindsay is quick to add to his discussion
of sculpture:

> I desire in the moving pictures, not the stillness but the
> majesty of sculpture. I do not advocate for the photoplay
> the mood of the Venus of Milo. But let us turn to that
> sister of hers, the great Victory of Samothrace, that
> spreads her wings at the head of the steps of the Louvre. . . .
> When you are appraising a new film, ask yourself: Is this
> motion as rapid, as god-like as the sweep of the wings of
> the Samothracian?[13]

Furthermore, he suggests that the serious student of the film look into
the history of sculpture for examples of classical figures which exhibit not the figure in repose but rather those which capture the
dynamism of some vigorous action. By noting and combining such figures
in the imagination, one might arrive at a better, more genuine action
picture than those which take their impetus and inspiration from, as he
puts it, "old stage material or newspaper clippings."[14] Speaking to the
film producer, Lindsay also suggests that if the film is to be improved,
its improvement will come about as a result of a thorough study of the
pictorial arrangement, with an eye toward "vitalized" sculpture.[15] Once
such figures are combined and imbued with movement it is possible to
attain that high state in the film which Lindsay characterizes as an
"orchestration of silent motion."[16] Yet this orchestration of motion
should not be of such intensity that its speed destroys the essential
beauty of the sculpturesque quality. Rather it should be such that the
audience is allowed the chance to savor the modelling. Inevitably
though, Lindsay returns to the supremacy of the pictorial element: "Let
any one section of the film, if it be stopped and studied, be grounded
in the same bronze conceptions."[17] It should be a type of filmic
sculpture which approximates the Michaelangelo figure in movement. Lindsay asks:

> Suppose the seated majesty of Moses should rise, what would
> be the quality of the action? Suppose the sleeping figures
> of the Medician tombs should wake, or those famous slaves
> should break their bands, or David again hurl the stone?
> Would not this action be as heroic as their quietness? Is
> it not possible to have a Michaelangelo of photoplay
> sculpture?[18]

Implicit here is a desire to imbue the film with more dignity, more of
the majesty and ageless quality of the masters of sculpture. It is

perhaps both a futile wish and an unwarranted comparison, yet it does
indicate Lindsay's effort to give to the film a modicum of respectability. Thus even though Lindsay inevitably returns to the purely
pictorial element of the classical sculpture, he is at the same time
genuinely concerned with the movement which they suggest. And it is
probable that he would be satisified with an action picture whose primary aim is movement for the sake of movement, provided that it carried
with it a pictorially pleasing sculptural quality. Of course, one
must never forget that uppermost in Lindsay's mind is a strict adherence
to the pictorial quality of the film. As he puts it,

> We go to the photoplay to enjoy right and splendid picture
> motions, to feel a certain thrill when the pieces of the
> kaleidoscope glass slide into new places. Instead of moving
> on straight lines, as they do in the mechanical toy, they
> progress in strange curves that are part of the very shapes
> into which they fall.19

It is significant that Lindsay reverses the term motion picture. And,
the full significance of this reversal becomes apparent when later in
the same work, The Art of the Moving Picture, he unequivocally states:
"If it is ever to evolve into a national art, it must first be good
picture, then good motion."20 It becomes apparent that Lindsay's prime
concern is with the graphic aspects of the film. That is, he must make
it clear in his own mind, and in the mind of the reader, that his
analysis is first and foremost a pictorial analysis of a medium which
has this new-found ability to capture motion. It is also quite probable
that his emphasis on the pictorial aspect is simply a reaction against
many of the films of his day, which were, in the purest sense of the
word, moving pictures. In other words, in 1915 many film makers were
still fascinated with movement for the sake of movement, with little

attention to any kind of pictorial artistry.

Thus far, Lindsay has concerned himself with only the sculptural figure and how best its lines, textures, planes, and nascent movement might be transfered to the photographic medium. His discussion has centered primarily around the beauty of the single figure. Lindsay does not, however, overlook completely the quality of sculpture which can derive from the grouping of a number of figures. In fact, the proper arrangement within the frame can lead to a form of perception unique to the film. As an example, he cites an interior scene which is filled with people. In such a case, Lindsay submits, the high relief of the various figures, as contrasted with the decor and furniture of the room, enables the eye to travel "not from space to space, or fabric to fabric, but first of all from mass to mass."[21] Thus, sculpture in motion also becomes a compositional construct which goes beyond a mere contemplation of the planal aspects of the individual figure.

In summary then, we find that the action photoplay is concerned, primarily, with physical force, speed, and the overall frenetic pace which arises from the chase episode. As a result if its preoccupation with this type of external action, the internal action of the photoplay, or the intellectual and emotional development of the characters, is compromised. The characters become, in a sense, mere pawns who serve to act out the obvious, oft-repeated plot line in which physical action is substituted for genuine dramatic intensity. Although Lindsay himself points out such shortcomings in the action picture, he is still able to find in it a vestige of hope. This hope comes from the fact that he chooses to superimpose over the action framework an artistic yardstick

called sculpture in motion which enables him to overlook the obvious
dramaturgical faults and see instead, the photographic beauties. Lindsay believes so strongly in the photographic beauty, and in this particular case, the plastic potential inherent in the film, that he holds
sculpture in motion to be a way in which the film will be able to
"transcend the narrow boundaries of the action picture."[22] The sculpturesque appearance of the action film comes from the fact that the
personages of the drama are often photographed in closeup, thus dis-
playing their linear and textural characteristics. And, it is from
this ability to display the plasticity of the figure that film derives
a part of its beauty and power. Although there is little doubt that
Lindsay is pictorially oriented, he does not neglect, completely, movement, one of the distinguishing characteristics of the film. In fact,
he suggests that the film maker look to statuary as a dynamic, rather
than a static resource.

This much is apparent in Lindsay's concept of sculpture in motion:
His art background is very definitely a factor in the way he views the
film. It is perhaps fair to say that art has been dragged in by the
heels and forcibly applied to the film as a standard of comparison.
Yet it is not applied so stringently as to overshadow the essential fact
that film is a genuinely dynamic art form rather than mere animated
gallery art. That is, one of the formative principles which distinguishes film from other pictorial arts, is that it is able to convey
continuous movement rather than merely "capturing" an isolated moment
in time as do painting and sculpture. It is obvious from his examples,
that Lindsay sees the realistic treatment of the figure in classical

sculpture as the most valuable model after which the film maker should

pattern his photography. It would seem that this choice of the real-

istic classical figure is, and must be, consistent with the photographic

realism of Lindsay's day. Otherwise, the two will not stand compar-

ison. Furthermore, it would seem that Lindsay's concern with the

"plastic sense" and the "high relief" of sculpture in motion, conveys

an interest not only in plasticity and movement for their own sake,

but in the illusion of depth which results from the photograph of the

plastic and moving figure. Thus sculpture in motion is not merely a

method for isolating a particular genre of film, but it too, like the

other motion concepts, is a principle by which one can isolate partic-

ular formal characteristics of the medium.

NOTES

[1] Lindsay, The Art. . . , p. 1.

[2] Ibid., p. 2.

[3] Ibid., p. 19.

[4] Ibid., p. 12.

[5] Ibid., p. 165.

[6] Ibid., p. 79.

[7] Lindsay, "The Greatest. . . ," Barrett Collection, p. 127.

[8] Ibid., p. 38.

[9] Lindsay, The Art. . . , p. 85.

[10] Ibid., p. 86.

[11] Lindsay, "Why I Think. . . ," Barrett Collection, p. 10.

[12] Lindsay, The Art. . . , p. 84.

[13] Ibid., p. 96.

[14] Ibid., p. 94.

[15] Ibid., p. 190.

[16] Lindsay, "The Greatest. . . ," Barrett Collection, p. 38.

[17] Lindsay, The Art. . . , p. 88.

[18] Ibid., p. 95.

[19] Ibid., p. 107.

[20]Ibid., p. 108

[21]Ibid., p. 91.

[22]Ibid., p. 96.

CHAPTER VI

Painting in Motion

In an effort to draw a broader, deeper-cutting distinction between the two genres, Lindsay compares the Intimate Photoplay (painting in motion) with the previously established category, the Action
Picture (sculpture in motion). As we have seen, the action picture
is that photoplay whose essential character is one of action which
is quite often shown to best advantage in the vast expanses of the
out-of-doors. The Intimate Photoplay, by way of contrast, is that
type which has its "photographic basis" in the "very small ground
plan and the cosiest of enclosing walls."[1] Thus, in the most literal
sense of the word, Lindsay uses physical restriction as the first
criterion of the intimate photoplay. Yet to understand the full meaning
of the intimate classification, one cannot be satisfied with a literal
acceptance of such phrases as "small ground plan," for Lindsay himself
does not stop here. From here, he progresses to a discussion of the
intimate photoplay or scene as one in which camera-to-subject distance
is relatively short when compared with the other two motion concepts,
sculpture and architecture. The concern seems to be with essences, or
an uncluttered photographic frame which includes only those aspects of
the composition necessary for total expression of the intended idea.
And in the intimate photoplay, people and their interactions seem to be
of the essence. For as Lindsay points out, the intimate motion picture
is a means whereby one may study the "half relaxed or gently restrained

moods of human creatures."[2] Such study is aided by the film's ability
to "move its audience" and to place it, photographically, in close
proximity to the characters on the screen. The closeup, to Lindsay,
carries with it a kind of empathic closeness. As he sees it:

> We in the audience are privileged characters. . . . We are
> members of the household on the screen. Sometimes we are
> sitting on the near side of the family board. Or we are
> gossiping, whispering neighbors, of the shoemaker, we will
> say, with our noses pressing against the pane of metaphoric
> window [of the shoeshop].[3]

Thus, regardless of how much Lindsay might like to reduce physical
distance, his efforts are frustrated by a metaphoric window which is no
doubt the same "fourth wall" which dramatic theorists have discussed for
more than two centuries. A further indication that the intimate motion
picture is concerned not only with restricted space, but with the
arrangement of the figure within the frame, can be found in Lindsay's
counter to the argument that the grandiose ballroom scene is an interior,
yet is in no way intimate. Lindsay neatly sidesteps the argument and
at the same time reinforces his contention that there is a certain intimacy which derives from the arrangement of small groups within the
frame:

> Masses of human beings pour by like waves, the personalities
> of none made plain. The only definite people are the hero
> and heroine in the foreground, and maybe one other. Though
> these three be in ball costume, the little triangle they
> occupy next to the camera is in sort, an interior. . . .[4]

Implicit here, and later stated, is the contention that the intimate
photoplay is best suited for small casts and that the film maker who
would make a truly intimate photoplay, must not attempt to film, for instance, "the whole big bloody plot of Lorna Doone."[5]

Interestingly enough, Lindsay realizes the restrictions he has placed upon his theoretical category by limiting it to the interior. Thus it is not suprising to find him admitting later, that the "intimate and friendly moving picture need not be indoors as long as it has the native hearth mood." Yet never completely retracting his original contention that the intimate photoplay has the "cosiness" of the interior, he continues by saying that "it is generally keyed to the hearth stone, and keeps quite close to it."[6]

Underlying Lindsay's entire discussion of the intimate photoplay is an implicit fondness for the intimate mood and all that it implies. Unfortunately though, such is an unrequited feeling, because as he points out, the majority of the films of his day were not of the intimate variety, but rather were more typically of the action type. However, with characteristic naive optimism, Lindsay sees hope for the intimate film in that there are, in his opinion, actors who fit the mood of the intimate photoplay. In fact, Lindsay's avowed devotion to Mary Pickford as one type who embodies the intimate mood, leads him to actually refer to the intimate film as that which has a sort of "Mary Pickford mood."[7]

By way of review then, we find Lindsay establishing a category for the intimate photoplay, which does not leave him with sufficient latitude for a full development of his own ideas. Consequently he is forced to retreat somewhat from his initial contention that the intimate photoplay is characterized by the interior scene. He first broadens the concept by asserting that examples of the intimate photoplay can also be found in the large interior provided the compositional

arrangement within the frame concentrates on the smaller, more important groups of people within the larger area. Finally, with an almost complete rejection of the original criteria, Lindsay clears away
all restrictions as to place by stating that the intimate mood may
also be achieved outdoors so long as it adheres to the mood of the
"hearth stone." Perhaps Lindsay's initial overstatement or rigid categorization can be explained by his desire to distinguish the intimate
from the other two motion concepts, sculpture and architecture, which
deal in large part, with vast spatial arrangements, and large numbers
of people. In the intimate picture, however, Lindsay's real concern
is with a more highly selective composition which clearly establishes
a small number of character relationships. Rather than being concerned
with a film which exhibits only excitement, suspense, or action for the
sake of action, Lindsay is interested in characterizing the intimate
photoplay as a genre whose function it is to depict people and their
passions.[8] Yet even this wish is frustrated by Lindsay himself, although perhaps not intentionally. Later in discussing another of the
motion concepts, architecture, Lindsay admits that "the motion picture
is shallow in showing private passion [but] it is powerful in conveying
the passions of masses of men."[9] Regardless of how much potential he
sees for the silent film, Lindsay is enough of the verbalist to admit
that such things as private romance or feeling "can only be traced by
the novelist, or by the gentle alternations of silence and speech on
the speaking stage, aided by the hot blood of the players actually before us."[10] If we then accept what Lindsay sees as the verbal limitations of the silent film, what does his theory grant as the proper

province of the intimate photoplay? It would appear that the answer to this question can be found in Lindsay's attempt to characterize those films of an "intimate" nature as examples of painting in motion. With this in mind, let us now turn to an examination of this relationship.

While pointing out that the concept of painting in motion is directly related to his chapter on the intimate photoplay, Lindsay also speaks of the idea of painting in motion as being "founded on the delicate effects that may be worked out from cosy interior scenes close to the camera."[11] It is at this point that his ceaseless devotion to the graphic arts as a standard of comparison for the film, becomes increasingly apparent. The words "delicate effects" in isolation are not striking ones, yet they seem to contain the key to a full understanding of the relationship between the intimate photoplay and painting in motion. For, once Lindsay embarks upon his analysis of painting in motion, his primary concern is with finding examples from the world of art which graphically illustrate the "delicate effects" possible in the moving image. His first concern is with the matter of relief, a term seldom applied to the analysis of a photographic work. Yet, the intimate photoplay, to Lindsay's way of thinking, is characteristically in "low relief."[12] What "low relief" implies here, is a concern with the two dimensions of the picture plane itself, rather than, as is the case with sculpture in motion, an interest in the "high relief" or apparent depth afforded by sculpture in motion.

From relief, Lindsay turns to a discussion of texture which results from the varying contrasts to be found in black and white photography.

The two terms, relief and texture, are used interchangeably to support
the contention that the intimate photoplay finds its best expression
when it is in low relief or lacking in tonal contrast. In other words,
Lindsay asks for a type of photographic rendering which is consonant
with the mood of the story or the particular scene depicted. This can
be seen in his description of a production still:

> Here is another sort of painting. The young mother in her
> pretty bed is smiling on her infant. The cot and covers and
> flesh tints have gentle scales of difference, all within
> one tone of the softest gray. Her hair is quite dark. It
> relates to the less luminous black of the coat of the physican
> behind the bed and the dress of the girl friend bending over
> her. The nurse standing by the door is a figure of the same
> gray-white as the bed. Within the pattern of the velvety-
> blacks there are as subtle gradations as in the pattern of
> the gray-whites. The tableau is a satisfying scheme in black
> and gray, with practically one non-obtrusive texture through-
> out.13

Thus it becomes increasingly apparent that the prime concern in painting in motion is with purely two dimensional perception. The concentration is upon the treatment of shape, space, and the subdued tonal contrasts of the flat picture plane. Lindsay also exhibits some concern
lest the added element of motion upset the delicate textural balance of
the action film:

> Let them take on motion without losing their charm or low
> relief, or their serene composition within the four walls
> of the frame. As for the motion, let it be a further ex-
> tension of the drawing. Let every gesture be a bolder, but
> not less graceful brush stroke.14

After making clear his position regarding the tonal qualities of
the successful intimate photoplay, Lindsay turns next to a cataloguing
of those art works which he feels could best serve as models for one
who would produce intimate photoplays.15 Such cataloguing is merely
a part of his method:

> Throughout this book I try to bring to bear the same simple standards of form, composition, mood, and motive that we used in finding fundamental exhibits; the standards which are taken for granted in art histories and schools, radical or conservative, anywhere.[16]

The intimate story could be told in the tone and with the brush work of

a Van Dyke; with "continence in nervous force" of a portrait by Manet;

with the illumination of a Charles W. Hawthorne portrait; with the

intimate humor of the Dutch Little Masters; or with the stateliness of

Gilbert Stuart's portrait of Washington.[17] It is to the American artist

James Whistler that Lindsay turns for a final look at what the intimate

photoplay should strive for:

> One view of the technique of this man might summarize it thus: fastidiousness in choice of subject, the picture well within the frame, low relief, a Velasquez study of tones and a Japanese study of spaces. . . . A Whistler, or a good Japanese print, might be described as a kaleidoscope suddenly arrested and transfixed at the moment of most exquisite relations in the pieces of glass. An intimate play of a kindred sort would start to turning the kaleidoscope again, losing fine relations only to gain those which are more exquisite and novel.[18]

Again we see demonstrated Lindsay's interest in the intimate photoplay

as a form which deals in low relief and subdued contrasts, thus pro-

ducing a type of film which is judged, primarily, on its two dimen-

sional merits. The point which should be noted from this listing of

prefered models, is that all of them, with the exception of Whistler,

are genre paintings which exhibit a definite mood, be it the state-

liness of the Washington portrait or the quiet intimacy of Gerard

Terburg's Music Lesson. In such paintings, Lindsay intimates, there

is a definite lesson for the film maker. If he will only "key" his

films to the moods of such paintings, success will be his--at least

to Lindsay's way of thinking.

At this point in his discussion of the concept of painting in motion, Lindsay brings forth a theoretical idea which he believes to be particularly applicable to the form of the intimate picture. He says, "All motion pictures might be characterized as <u>space measured without sound</u>, <u>plus time measured without sound</u>."[19] At first glance this succinct characterization of the motion picture appears to be a comprehensive statement of the film's ability to either compress or extend time and space--a capability which later film theorists point to as one of the formative principles of the medium. Yet closer examination reveals that Lindsay exhibits an understand of, or at least chooses to discuss, only the concept of time measured without sound. Rather than treat space measured without sound as an editing technique which enables film instantaneously to move its viewer through geographic space, Lindsay treats it as the actual space within the confines of the frame. In other words, space measured without sound becomes a composition construct which deals with the arrangement of forms within the individual frame, rather than one which grapples with the more pertinent and illuminating issue of the difference between time and space in film, and time and space in reality. Lindsay's reluctance to discuss space as a concept inextricably linked to time is probably not a result of ignorance of the concept, but rather can be explained by his pervasive interest in the two dimensional aspect of painting in motion. One explanation for this consuming interest in pictorial composition lies in Lindsay's unequivocal statement that if film is "ever to evolve into a national art, it must first be good picture, then good motion";[20] a rationale arrived at as a result of some dangerously faulty logic:

"first come the photograph. Then motion was added to the photograph. We must use this order in our judgement."[21] Such logic is faulty for the simple reason that in film, motion and picture are inseparables in that motion is a part of composition.

Although Lindsay says that it is "harder to grasp" the other half of the total concept, i.e., time measured without sound, it is interesting to note that it is this very half of the concept which receives a far more sophisticated and knowledgeable treatment. In a metaphoric vein which is typical of The Art of the Moving Picture, he states:

> Think of a lively and humoresque clock that does not tick and takes only an hour to record a day. Think of a noiseless electric vehicle, where you are looking out of the windows, going down the smooth boulevard of Wonderland. Consider a film with three simple time elements; (1) that of the pursuer, (2) the pursued, (3) the observation vehicle of the camera following the road and watching both of them, now faster, now slower than they, as the photographer overtakes the actors or allows them to hurry ahead.[22]

Outlined here is the essence of filmic time; a time which can be manipulated at the discretion of the film maker or by what the context of the film itself dictates. In the metaphor of the clock we have stated for us the compression of time, and in the temporal breakdown of the chase is outlined the extension of time. But, Lindsay has great difficulty in refraining from a reversion to a discussion of the pictorial aspect of time measured without sound. Thus, he appends to the broader concept of time continuum, a detailed description of the function of time flux as a technique of composition:

> No two people in the same room should gesture at one mechanical rate, or like their forks or spoons, keeping obviously together. Yet it stands to reason that each successive tableau should be not only a charming picture, but the totals of should be an orchestration of various speeds, of abrupt, graceful, and seemingly awkward progress, worked into a silent symphony.[23]

Also hinted at in the above is the overall tempo of the film which is, at least partially, a result of editing. In a manner which sounds much like the theories of Sergei Eisenstein which were to come some fifteen years later, Lindsay speaks of time as a tool of composition:

> In the background, the waves toss in one tempo. Owing to the sail, the boat rocks in another. In the foreground the tree alternately bends and recovers itself in the breeze, making more opposition than the sail.[24]

For all its sophistication, the theory of space and time measured without sound offers one of the more glowing contradictions of the book. As was mentioned earlier, Lindsay says that the concept offers a way to describe all films, but it is a description which "fits in a special way the delicate form"[25] of the intimate picture. The contradiction arises out of Lindsay's choice of what is obviously an example from an action picture rather than an intimate picture. That is, the chase episode which he uses to illustrate the various time levels is precisely the element which he has isolated as being a distinctive characteristic of the action picture. Thus if we accept Lindsay's intimate genre as delicate and subdued, then this chase element hardly measures up as either delicate or subdued. On the other hand, Lindsay's treatment of space as the delicate measurement of space within the frame, more closely approximates what we have come to recognize as the mood of the intimate picture. In other words, it would appear that he has tailored this half of the concept to fit the intimate genre. But, in order to make his discussion of the time flux a meaningful and obvious one, he has chosen the most patently obvious example of time flux, the chase. One question still remains unanswered, however, and that is why Lindsay chooses to discuss this theoretical idea in the context of the intimate

film, rather than in one of the other two concepts. His only comment is
that in the context of the intimate genre, the concept "can be studied
out, free from irrelevant issues."[26] Just what these irrelevant issues
are, is never made clear.

Any attempt to summarize Lindsay's intimate photoplay and its
artistic corollary painting in motion, forces one into the tenous position
of attempting to unravel his ofttimes twisted train of thought. By initially overstating his case in an attempt to draw deep distinctions
among the other motion constructs, and also by attempting to emphasize
the supremacy of picture, Lindsay makes the problem of determining the
precise meaning of the intimate category extremely difficult for both
himself and his reader. The initial reaction is that Lindsay is concerned with isolating a type of photoplay whose essential nature is
characterized by restricted interior spaces and the intimacy which
comes from the arrangement of small groups of actors within the context
of larger groups, when in reality the true goal of the intimate picture
is "the transformation of the actors."[27] Lindsay, it appears, is quick
to realize that any such transformation can be brought about by locale
and composition alone. It must, as he suggests in a later work, be a
transformation which results from the work of the actors themselves; a
transformation which can come only from the subtle gesture, the elusive
facial expression and all of the other aspects of the immaterial which
go to make up the story. In his words, the intimate photoplay "is not
epic, but, as it were, lyric."[28] Of course it is hardly possible to
convey the lyric mood by means of an epic vehicle. And, it is tenable
that such is Lindsay's point--the only problem being that he discusses

first the vehicle, then the mood. It is only when he attempts to wed

the intimate mood to his own category of painting in motion that he con-

cedes his mistake and is forced to view the intimate photoplay as one

whose overall effect is akin to the mood of the intimate, subdued, and

restrained painting. This, of course, allows him all the latitude that

is needed, for a painting can elicit a certain restraint and subtlety

regardless of whether it be a single figure or the limitless groups of

the truly monumental painting. In a word, the intimate mood of either

a painting or a film comes not so much from what is depicted, but rather

from the way in which it is depicted. At least this appears to be

Lindsay's position. Evidence of this viewpoint can be seen in a specific

example from the film The Thief of Bagdad:

> This caravansary [three marching princes with retinue] is a good
> example of painting in motion, perhaps in the most extreme
> illustration in motion pictures to be completely successful. In
> the midst of the interminable desert sand arises one lonely cliff-
> like rock, like the enchanted mesa of the south west, with a path
> winding up, that is reminiscent of the tower of Babel, in the
> Sunday school picture books of our childhood.[29]

Thus in this one illustration, Lindsay has denied all the principles laid

down for the intimate photoplay--the interior, the small group, the trans-

formation of the actors, the native hearth mood--yet the scene is an ex-

ample of painting in motion. It appears that the best explanation for

this gross contradiction lies in the fact that Lindsay has superimposed

upon certain films and parts of films, the criteria of painting in

motion--delicate and subtle tonal values, controlled two dimensional

composition--and then has worked backwards toward a rationale of content.

In fact, the multiplicity of contradictions and inconsistencies which

occur in Lindsay's discussion leads to an inevitable conclusion:

Painting in motion is a formative principle of the film rather than a
guide for isolating any one specific genre of film. Regardless of how
hard Lindsay tries to isolate a particular genre as being representative
of painting in motion, he inevitably contradicts himself with an example which in no way resembles the genres which he has discussed.
Thus the concept of painting in motion is a formative principle which is
concerned with, to use Lindsay's term, an "intimate" technique rather
than an intimate genre. This "intimate" technique is one in which the
prime concern is with the two dimensional characteristics of the film.
As opposed to sculpture in motion, in which the illusion of depth is the
controlling element, Lindsay's concern here is with the pleasing
arrangement of forms, space, and subdued tonal values on the picture
plane. In the final analysis, perhaps the best way to determine Lindsay's primary formative concern is always to look at the traditional art
form which he uses as a standard of comparison. By looking at the
traditional art form which he uses, not only can one determine the
formative elements of the film which are being subjected to close examination, but again one can see that Lindsay's background in the
graphic and plastic arts is very much in evidence as he goes about his
structural analysis of the film.

NOTES

[1] Lindsay, The Art. . . , p. 19.

[2] Ibid., p. 21.

[3] Ibid., p. 20.

[4] Ibid., p. 21.

[5] Ibid., p. 22.

[6] Ibid., p. 99.

[7] Ibid., p. 26.

[8] Ibid., p. 21.

[9] Ibid., p. 40

[10] Ibid., p. 52.

[11] Ibid., p. 97.

[12] Ibid.

[13] Ibid., p. 99.

[14] Ibid., p. 101.

[15] Ibid., pp. 101-106.

[16] Ibid., p. 19.

[17] Ibid., pp. 101-105.

[18] Ibid., p. 106.

[19] Ibid.

[20] Ibid., p. 108.

[21] Ibid., pp. 107-108.

[22] Ibid., p. 109.

[23] Ibid., p. 110.

[24] Ibid.

[25] Ibid., p. 106.

[26] Ibid., p. 107.

[27] Ibid., p. 112.

[28] Lindsay, The Greatest. . . ," Barrett Collection, p. 128.

[29] Ibid., p. 74.

CHAPTER VII

Architecture in Motion

Just as in the case of sculpture in motion and painting in motion,
Lindsay first outlines what he takes to be the essential nature of the
film genre which exhibits architecture characteristics. This genre,
designed as the splendor picture, is broken down into four different
forms, each of which overlaps the other three. However, these four
forms, regardless of what differences and similarities they might
possess, are all based on the fact that the film can, as Lindsay puts
it,

> . . . take in the most varied of out-of-door landscapes. It can
> reproduce fairy dells. It can give every ripple of the lily pond.
> It can show us cathedrals within and without. It can take in the
> panorama of cyclopean cloud, bending forest, stormhung mountain.
> In like manner it can put on the screen great impersonal mobs of
> men. It can give us tremendous armies, moving as oceans move.[1]

The four genres, fairy splendor, crowd splendor, patriotic splendor,
and religious splendor embody the above capabilities. This chapter
will treat them in the above order, which is the order dictated by
Lindsay.

Of the four generic terms, fairy splendor, at first glance, appears to be the most literal in meaning, because Lindsay is, in fact,
speaking of the film's ability to deal with the supernatural. But,
Lindsay is consistently inconsistent, and later uses the term to describe something other than the purely supernatural film. For now,
however, let us examine the literal meaning of the term. The camera, as
Lindsay sees it, has a "kind of Halloween witch-power,"[2] which allows it
to manipulate and distort reality to fit the demands of the fairy tale.

Although the film eventually may be able to reveal the old world leg-
ends, fairy tales, and man's relation to nature, for the present we
should look to the simple Mother Goose rhyme for the basic photoplay.
In the famous lines, "Rat will not gnaw rope / Rope will not hang
butcher" is found, according to Lindsay, the basic elements for the
photoplay of fairy splendor.[3] It is his contention that man, throughout history, has always imbued objects with human characteristics.
Arthur, for instance, names his blade Excalibur and it becomes a person
to him. Likewise the man in the Arabian nights tale speaks of his
carpet and it becomes his slave, performing for him a transportation
function. Thus the motion picture of fairy splendor can fulfill a
fantasy function which heretofore has been restricted to the world of
literary fiction.

As an example of the way in which the motion picture of fairy
splendor can captivate an audience and at the same time, capitalize on
its desire for objects which act, Lindsay cites a French film entitled
Moving Day in which the principle action of the plot is carried out by
invisible characters. In this film, built around moving day in a
typical household, empty shoes stroll down the street, and into the new
home. The ability to perform this sort of legerdemain is, to Lindsay's
way of thinking, "fundamental to the destinies of the art."[4] Yet, he
submits, this sort of production is being neglected because movie producers are convinced that people do not enjoy being put upon by such
trickery. Lindsay insists, however, that audiences object only to
trickery for the sake of trickery, but are unflagging in their desire
for any such plot which stimulates the imagination. The way to success

in this sort of film is to allow the objects to take on their own

character and become the principle actors rather than sublimating them

to a position secondary to the human actor.[5] Thus we arrive at what

appears to be the essential feature of the splendor picture--anthropo-

morphism. Although the idea of objects as actors is one which runs

throughout Lindsay's entire discussion of splendor pictures, and in

fact the entire book, it nevertheless receives its first clear expres-

sion in his discussion of the photoplay of fairy splendor. For a more

complete development of the idea, let us turn to the chapter which

Lindsay calls the corollary of the film of fairy splendor, "Furniture,

Trappings and Inventions in Motion."

Although he sees it as worthy of a separate chapter, the fairy

splendor picture and its corresponding movement concept are still in-

cluded under the general head of architecture in motion. Such a clas-

sification is justified, according to Lindsay, simply because furniture

and furniture-making are often discussed as sub-categories of archi-

tecture. Returning to the idea of the inanimate being imbued with

movement or human characteristics, Lindsay admits that a film which is

made up of a meaningless group of tricks or special effects, is nothing

more than a nuisance. When and only when tricks are given an essential

dignity and made "thoughts in motion and made visible,"[6] are they of

any artistic value. For instance in Moving Day, the film described

above, the shoes should be made the principal actors in order that they

might call to mind such classic fairy tales as The Seven Leagued Boots,

The Enchanted Moccasins, Puss in Boots and Cinderella.[7] So strongly does Lindsay believe that the object should take its place as an actor that he suggests Cinderella's slipper as the real heroine of the film story. This, of course, leaves little doubt that fairy splendor is at once a literal term used to describe a certain genre of film, and a term which is also used as a springboard for the much broader notion of anthropomorphism.

To understand fully, Lindsay's concept of anthropomorphism it is first necessary to examine the philosophy which underlies his notion of what constitutes the fairy tale. Lindsay holds: "Substitution is not the fairy story. It is transformation, transfiguration, that is the fairy story, be it a divine or a diabolical change."[8] Thus it seems tenable that Lindsay views those objects which become actors not as mere substitutes for persons, but as transformations which embody the complete behavioral pattern of the person for which they stand. For instance, it would not be enough to let shoes simply represent Cinderella; they must conjure up in the mind of the viewer the very essence of the entire character of Cinderella, and the entire idea behind her story. In other words, Lindsay's idea of anthropomorphism transcends simple association of an inanimate object with a particular character. Rather it should be, as he intimates, a transference of the totality of the character to the appropriate object. It is here, that Lindsay alludes to his concept of hieroglyphics which will be dealt with in a later chapter. For the moment, however, let it suffice to say that Lindsay's hieroglyphics concept is also concerned with symbolism through objects. There is little doubt that the two concepts anthropomorphism and hieroglyphics, are inextricably linked, thus

Lindsay finds it difficult not to at least mention hieroglyphics at
this point. Fairy splendor is then, as Lindsay puts it, "furniture
transfigured, for without transfiguration there is no spiritual motion
of any kind."[9] Of course, a paradox arises when one chooses to speak
of the picture of fairy splendor as furniture transfigured and at the
same time continues to use, as the prime example, Cinderella's shoe.
This, it would seem, is another indication of the metaphoric quality of
Lindsay's approach in the entire book. He seems to take considerable
freedom with his own terms, and enlarges them to fit the occasion at
hand. In this case, it is reasonable to assume that shoes fall under
the heading of "trappings." Be that as it may, the important thing is
that all inanimate objects, be they furniture, trappings, or inventions,
are, or at least should be, invested with life in order that they may
take their proper place as actors within the film.

To appreciate fully, the position which objects hold in Lindsay's
theory, it might be well to cite a few of the examples which he gives.

D. W. Griffith's Avenging Conscience, an adaptation of Edgar Allen
Poe's The Tell Tale Heart contains excellent examples of what Lindsay
describes as furniture, trappings, and inventions in motion. After the
murderer has been apprehended and is being questioned by the police,
the objects and people around him begin to produce acute examples of
objects in motion. First, the incessant tapping of the detective's
pencil in time with the beating of the heart, becomes a form of
furniture in motion and likewise, the rhythmic tapping of the shoe and
the swing of the clock pendulum, forms of trappings and inventions in
motion.[10] It is perhaps even more important to see how Lindsay

visualizes these objects and their effects:

> Here more unearthliness hovers round a pendulum than any merely
> mechanical trick movements could impart. Then the merest common-
> place of the detective tapping his pencil in the same time--the
> boy trying in vain to ignore it--increases the strain, till the
> audience has well nigh the hallucinations of the victim. Then
> the bold tapping of the detective's foot, who would do all his
> accusing without saying a word, and the startling coincidence
> of the owl hoot-hooting outside the window to the same measures,
> bring us close to the final breakdown. These realistic material
> actors are as potent as the actual apparations of the dead man
> that preceded them. Those visions prepared the mind to invest
> trifles with significance.[11]

In his later work, "The Greatest Movies Now Running," Lindsay continues

to hold to this position when he describes a scene from the film

Covered Wagon. In this film, there is a scene in which the husband

suggests to his wife that they leave behind her grandmother's bureau

in order that the wagon's load might be lightened. The wife vehemently

objects to this suggestion on the grounds that the piece of furniture

is a family heirloom. Of this incident in the film, Lindsay says:

> No better illustration could be found of what I mean when I say
> that in the movies inanimate things become animate and become
> the principle actors. For a hundred years, sentiment and dream
> had centered around this homelike bit of furniture and surely
> after that many years had been poured into it for significance,
> it has a right to speak for itself, and for all those who had
> lived and died in its presence. It was in itself a sort of
> chariot or wagon train of dreamland. It carried in itself
> multitudinous seeds and slips from an old fashioned garden in
> the East, of flowers which were themselves hereditary.[12]

Thus it is apparent that objects do, indeed, take on symbolic charac-

teristics which recall to the audience not only the character which

they represent, but the inner workings of both the character and the

context in which he operates. It should also be noted that Lindsay

holds the view that not only he, but all movie audiences are aware of

and appreciate the anthropomorphic quality of the film. He contends that movie audiences have been "thoroughly trained to expect inanimate

things to become actors."[13] And in cosmic terms, Lindsay insists that

this training is a result of one of the irrefutable facts of the film:

> It [the film] is the setting in motion of things which we have
> assumed were forever motionless. It is like that first revelation
> to ignorant humanity that the earth is whirling in a dizzy circuit
> around the sun with the various planets, and the conception that
> all the universe is likewise whirling through space. This dancing
> of the spheres has now become the motion and the heroism of the
> parlor furniture. Since the photoplay art is the only art in the
> world by which things can at last assert their personality,
> certainly things have the right of way there. It is their first
> and last chance to act. Let them, as it were, the first and last
> time in any art, impersonate and cartoon themselves. Let them
> be sent on their way to show us, by such gestures as they can,
> their real meaning for us. Let the hieroglyphics indeed march
> and sing, and let those human beings who have thought they have
> enslaved them for so long, subordinate themselves for a little
> while and then cast their eyes about, and discern the actual
> natural rhythm of all things that seem inanimate, from the rope
> to the flying carpet.[14]

Thus the film, because of this basic propensity to set things in motion,

naturally gravitates toward objects and ideas which are photographable.

As an instance of this, Lindsay cites a Civil War film in which the

bulk of the action centers around the capture of a locomotive which

"took on more personality in the end than private or General on either

side, alive or dead."[15] This "personality" of which Lindsay speaks is

not limited to recognizable man-made objects around which the plot and

action center. Indeed, objects may even assume no other function than

one of pure decorative design, which, according to Lindsay, gives to

film a sort of seductive vitality. Nature too, comes into play in the

anthropomorphic concept. So much so, that when the non-human object

is of natural origin, it becomes pantheistic and speaks for all

nature.[16] The sea, for instance, can become the main actor in the film.[17]

Turning to the second of the splendor genres, the picture of crowd splendor, here is what Lindsay says of the crowd and its function in the film:

> It was generally conceded long ago that the crowd was a funda-
> mental actor in the movies, far more than on the stage. Griffith
> developed this idea with tremendous power in The Birth of A Nation
> and in Intolerance, the two most vital and leavening of all the
> old movies. From these two movies, all others have been derived.[18]

Initially then, Lindsay uses the term crowd splendor as a literal one. His approach, however, is circuitous. First, he holds that one of the fundamental resources of the silent film is its ability to convey the nobility of the sea. And since this is a fundamental resource of the film, almost any film maker is capable of doing a reasonably good job in presenting this natural phenomenon. However, and this is the essential point, only the master of the silent film such as Griffith is capable of presenting the sea of humanity.[19] Thus the mere craftsman can present the sea as a part of the natural order, but genuine art-istry is necessary to present its metaphoric counterpart, the sea of humanity.

It is in presenting this sea of humanity that film finds its par-ticular power. As Lindsay suggests throughout his writing, film is particularly limited in its ability to portray the development of, as he puts it "private passions." That is, the silent film, because it is silent, is hard put to disclose the subtle inner workings of the single character's mind as he grapples with his individual or "private" pro-blems. However, through the visual element alone, the film is capable of establishing character relationships. It is the enlargement of this idea that Lindsay sees as one of its greatest powers. Film, Lindsay

suggests, may be ever so "shallow" in presenting the private passions

yet it is powerful in "conveying the passions of masses of men."[20]

Comparing it to literature, he finds the film nearest the epic and the

narrative in form. Of course the film derives its epic nature from the

very fact that it can present crowds of monumental proportions. The

film crowd, to Lindsay's way of thinking and seeing, assumes its own

peculiar character just as the inanimate objects made actors take on

their own individual personalities. For example, in his discussion

of particular films which are most representative of his idea of the

picture of crowd splendor, Lindsay sees each crowd scene as having its

own unique character and mood. It would seem that the importance of

this idea lies not in the unique character of the crowd but rather in

Lindsay's notion that within each of these crowds there are characters

who express not only their own thoughts and actions, but those of the

entire group. In other words, throughout his discussion of the crowd

picture Lindsay appears to be speaking of a _pars pro toto_ concept.

That this is true becomes evident in his analysis of The Italian, a

Thomas Ince production. The immigrant hero of this film, according to

Lindsay, represents not merely his own individual problems, but those

of the "whole Italian race coming to America: its natural southern

gayety set in contrast to the drab East Side. The gondolier becomes

boot black. The grape-gathering peasant girl becomes the suffering

slum mother. They are not specialized characters like Pendennis or

Becky Sharp in the novels of Thackeray."[21] In fact, it is this very

generalized characterization which often gives the film its impact,

although the viewer often does not recognize the general nature of the
individual character:

> If you go to a motion picture and feel yourself suddenly gripped
> by the highest dramatic tension, as on the old stage, and re-
> flect afterward that it was a fight between only two or three
> men in a room otherwise empty, stop and analyze what they stood
> for. They were probably representatives of groups or races that
> had been pursuing each other earlier in the film.[22]

The individual as representative of the mass is perhaps best illus-

trated, to Lindsay's way of thinking, in D. W. Griffith's Birth of a

Nation. Here, the white leader, Ben Cameron is not simply an isolated

individual within the context of the film, but rather is the filmic

representation of the entire Anglo-Saxon race. By the same token, the

audience in Ford's theatre during the assasination scene, is repre-

sented by two young people in seats nearest the camera. Thus, they

and Cameron take on a visualizing function which goes beyond their own

individuality into the realm of the mass which they represent.

The third type of splendor picture, the picture of patriotic

splendor, need not be epic in proportion, although it sometimes is.

So long as it is truly patriotic in theme, then it measures up as a

part of the genre. Like the other splendor genres, the essence of the

patriotic film seems to be in its ability to portray, through the in-

dividual, the idea of the mass; the basic difference being in the idea

presented. Here, of course, the primary concern is with conveying a

sense of patriotism. In this respect, Lindsay holds that one in-

dividual within the film can represent the nationalistic spirit of the

entire nation from which he comes. For example, in The Typhoon, pro-

duced by Thomas Ince, Sessue Hayakawa becomes the representative of the

Japanese nation, regardless of whether he appears as a representative
of the crowd or alone.[23] In other words, within the context of this
particular film, he becomes the single dominant symbol for the entire
nation. This, it would seem, indicates that the idea of pars pro toto
is closely related to the concept of hieroglyphics, which will be
treated later in this investigation.

In the D. W. Griffith production of Judith of Bethulia, which Lindsay sees as a prime example of the picture of patriotic splendor, the
two lovers, Nathan and Naomi are brilliant examples of how two indi-
viduals can stand as representatives of the mass. In his words, "they
are generally doing the things the crowd behind them is doing, meanwhile
evolving their own little heart affair."[24] However, the power of this
particular film does not stop with the simple portrayal of the two
lovers. It is Lindsay's contention that this film is truly indicative
of what the film art can and should do in terms of the true patriotic
spirit:

> Though in this story the archaic flavor is well preserved, the way
> the producer has pictured the population at peace, in battle, in
> despair, in victory gives me hope that he or men like unto him will
> illustrate the American patriotic crowd-prophecies. We must have
> Whitmanesque scenarios, based on the moods akin to that of the poem
> By Blue Ontario's Shore. The possibility of showing the entire
> American population its own face in the Mirror Screen has at least
> come. Whitman brought the idea of democracy to our sophisticated
> literati, but did not persuade the democracy itself to read his
> democratic poems. Sooner or later the kinetoscope will do what he
> could not, bring the nobler side of the equality idea to the
> people who are so crassly equal.25

Thus it becomes apparent that the crowd picture, and particularly
the picture of patriotic splendor, has the power to illustrate for the
country as a whole, the true American spirit; or at least what Lindsay

sees as the true Americanism. Film is best suited to this social mission mainly because it is a mass art which "penetrates in our land to the haunts of the wildest or the dullest."[26] The man who leads the most insular existence is able to see the same films that are displayed on Broadway, therefore enabling the entire country to see the same films, and, hopefully, think the same patriotic thoughts; thoughts which remind the viewers of their own nationality in the fullest sense of the word. And finally, Lindsay sees the film as having a unifying effect which goes far beyond national boundaries: "We Americans should look for the great photoplay of tomorrow, that will mark a decade or a century, that prophesies of the flags made one, the crowds in brotherhood."[27]

Religious splendor, the fourth and final splendor genre is, like the rest, a form of crowd emotion, but a particular kind of crowd emotion which lends itself to the filmic presentation of the religious ritual. Lindsay holds that all of the splendor genres, because they deal with masses of people, are particularly suited to the film. Yet when he speaks of the picture of religious splendor he becomes vehement and more specific about the film being the best place to present the picture of crowd emotion. He says: "In the most conventional and rigid church sense this phase [religious splendor] can be conveyed more adequately by the motion picture than by the stage."[28] Perhaps because of his own strong religious background, and his reverence for the ex- ternals of faith, it is Lindsay's opinion that a direct transference of things religious to the screen will, by their very nature, be impressive or make impressive films of religious splendor. This feeling is clearly exhibited in his discussion of The Death of Thomas Becket, which, in

terms of technique, hardly measured up as a good film. Nevertheless,
Lindsay admits to being deeply moved during Becket's death scene which
he describes as "one of the few deaths in moving pictures that have
given me the sense that I was watching a tragedy."[29] Other death
scenes, if they have any effect at all, usually remind him of the death
scenes in oil paintings. The viewer feels, perhaps, a certain degree of
admiration for the technique of the painting, but little genuine emotion
for the action portrayed. On the other hand, the film version of
Becket's death was impressive because of the epic proportions which it
assumed: "The church procession, the robes, the candles, the vaulting
overhead, the whole visualized cathedral mood has the power over the
reverent eye it has in life, and a touch more."[30] In discussing this
issue of the film of religious splendor, Lindsay returns to a point
made earlier in the work, this being that private emotions are seldom,
if ever, effective in the film. The same is true in the case of the
picture of religious splendor. However, the distinguishing factor in
the case of Becket, lies in the fact that he is a public figure who is
accorded a considerable degree of respect and admiration. Hence Lindsay's idea of what constitutes tragedy in the film, is not unlike the
Aristotelian concept of tragedy. Added to this tragic view is Lindsay's
avowed fondness for ritual, which he feels is the quintessence of the
photoplay of religious splendor.

As an example, in fact the only example, of the kind of ritualistic
presentation which the film is so well equipped to portray, Lindsay
refers to the production Battle Hymn of the Republic. He admits that
this film, if taken literally, is probably best characterized as one of

blatant patriotism. But, as he interprets it, the film is possessed by
"so marked a devotion,"[31] that it becomes an illustration of the
religious photoplay. Apparently what leads him to this assertion is the
director's literal visualization of the song of the same name. First,
Julia Ward Howe is shown rising from her bed and writing the Battle
Hymn. As the lyrics pour forth, so do the visual images which might
have passed through her mind. For example, as the lines "Mine eyes have
seen the glory of the coming of the Lord" are flashed upon the screen,
there appears next, a picture of the nativity. These "visible parables"
as Lindsay calls them, continue through the writing of the poem. Today,
such patent visualization would no doubt be considered something less
than masterly, yet Lindsay sees in this sequence, "a tableau that proves
the motion picture a great religious instrument."[32] And too, it serves
as an illustration of "ritualistic birth, death, and resurrection."[33]
Thus the film maker, if he will but capitalize on the powers inherent
in the film, can preach, or at least present for his viewers, the
religious splendor so necessary for a healthy America. As Lindsay puts
it, "the faculty for commanding the great spirits of history and making
visible the unseen powers of the air, should be applied to the crowd
pictures which interpret the non-sectarian prayers of the broad human
race."[34]

Hence, in this genre, the genre of religious splendor, we can see
the effect of Lindsay's religious background. He views this type of
picture as a means whereby the film maker is able to benefit his
audience by making use of the art, beauty, religion triad which was
discussed in Chapters III and IV of this study. Furthermore, not only

can religious revelation come from the beauty of the formative elements

of the film, but as in the case of the film of religious splendor, it

can come from the subject matter treated, or if you will, by means of

"direct preaching." At work in Lindsay's analysis of this genre is his

background in art and religion, and his hope for a film of social

utility.

The underlying foundation of the concept of architecture in motion

can be found in Lindsay's fondness for basing his theory and evaluation

of the film on accepted principles within the other art forms; in this

case the purely formal aspects of the graphic arts. As was mentioned

earlier, Lindsay contends that in the film, "non-human tones, textures,

lines and spaces take on a vitality almost like that of flesh and

blood."[35] Basing his case on this assumption, Lindsay further argues

that since film gives a certain life-like vitality to line, texture,

and space, the ideal person to produce the finer photoplay is not neces-

sarily the person trained in the theatre but rather, young painters,

sculptors, and architects who are willing and eager to experiment with

the medium. Finally, of these three groups, the architect is best

qualified to "advance the work in the ultra-creative photoplay."[36]

At this point, the question arises, why is the architect better

suited for this mission than the painter or the sculptor? One possible

answer to this question lies in the fact that Lindsay equates the

splendorous with the monumental. That is, since the splendor picture is

basically a crowd genre it therefore requires a creator who is capable

of dealing with large masses, be they people or objects. Hence the

architect qualifies because of his ability to handle mass, line, texture,

and space. As Lindsay puts it: "In the arrangement of crowds and flow
of costuming and study of tableau climaxes, let the architect bring an
illusion of that delicate flowering, that brilliant instant of time
before the Peloponnesian war."[37] Enlarging upon this obvious preference
for the classical mood, Lindsay suggests further that the principle
figure of such a photoplay be Athena, who like the crowds around her,
should resemble a great pillar. Further, "the crowds should be like the
tossing waves of the Ionic Sea and Athena like the white ship upon the
waves.[38] The fact that Lindsay speaks in what might be termed "architectural similies" can best be explained by his attempt to emphasize
not the fact that Athena, or any character for that matter, actually
looks like a pillar, but that the lines which emanate from the character
carry with them the stateliness, and the reserve of the typical classical composition. In other words, the architect-film maker should use as
his model, the principles of mural painting; models such as the works
of Puvis de Chavannes whose distinction lies in his use of the extended
horizontal and perpendicular line.[39] Although linear relationships seem
to be the focus of Lindsay's attention, he is quick to add that action
is still important to the idea of architecture in motion and that
perhaps one of the best examples of the mural painting of action can be
found in the murals of Tintoretto.[40]

Becoming more specific, Lindsay analyzes for his reader, the linear
aspects of a production still taken from a movie magazine:

> For a crowd picture, for instance, here is a scene at a masquerade
> ball. The glitter of the costumes is an extension of the glitter
> of the candelabra overhead. The people are as it were chandeliers,
> hung lower down. The lines of the candelabra relate to the very
> ribbon streamers of the heroine, and the massive wood work is the

big brother of the square shouldered heroes in the foreground. . . .[41]

In a similar fashion he exhibits an interest in not only line, but in

the effect of light and shade on the "architectural characteristics" of

the film:

> Here is a night picture from a war story in which the light is
> furnished by two fires whose coals and brands are hidden by earth
> heaped in front. . . . The far end of the line of those keeping
> bivouac disappears into the distance, and the depths of the ranks
> behind them fade into the thick shadows. The flag, a little above
> the line, catches the light. One great tree overhead spreads its
> leafless half-lit arms through the gloom. Behind this is un-
> mitigated black. The composition reminds one of a Hiroshige study
> of midnight. These men are certainly a part of the architecture
> of out-of-doors. . . .[42]

The means by which the film maker may create and control these

essential elements of line, texture and space, is outlined by Lindsay

in an extended discussion of a hypothetical film scenario of the life

of Joan of Arc. This discussion carries various examples of how

Tintoretto evolved his composition and lighting through the use of

models, and how the film maker if he will but use the same procedures,

might also create a classic film. In addition, he suggests what he

considers to be the finest architecture throughout the world, from

which the film maker could take his inspiration.

In the main, Lindsay's discussion of the concept of architecture

in motion is even more metaphorical than his treatment of the other two

motion concepts. Yet, he inevitably returns, at one point or another,

to a discussion which bears on the literal meaning of the word archi-

tecture. For instance, he speaks of actual films <u>about</u> architecture,

rather than films which simply exhibit the compositional character,

line, texture, and mass of architecture. In other words, it is his

feeling that if more films were made which delineated the best in architecture, they could then be used as models upon which cities and towns could pattern themselves.[43] Perhaps what best sums up Lindsay's notion of what falls under the head of architecture in motion is his own reaction to The Thief of Bagdad:

> Go the next two times for architecture in motion, that is, see the great towers of each city moved by . . . note how while on the extraordinary flying carpet which you, yourself, seem to ride like a flying machine, the buildings and streets of the city pour by like real actors. Stars and clouds pile up into architecture and becomes actors. This great fundamental resource of the photoplay, architecture in motion, can be illustrated for you these two times, each time with amazing novelties. For instance, you can spend one whole evening just watching stairways and see how they seem to leap like race horses from scene to scene, or pour like cataracts through the various archways. The stairways of The Thief of Bagdad are magnificent actors.[44]

For all his talk of line, texture, and space, Lindsay still retains an interest in pure movement. Here, however, it is movement which is imparted to objects through the actual movement of the camera, rather than movement in front of the camera, as in the action picture, or sculpture in motion.

Viewed as a group, the four splendor genres encompass a broad area of content ranging from the film of fantasy to that of pure crowd splendor. Although the difference types of films are discussed under the different genres, each shares with the other a common element, the crowd. These films, although similar in method, differ in theme. There are pictures of religious or ritualistic intent, those which are patriotic in tone, and those which simply deal with large masses of people and thus assume epic proportions.

In his discussion of the film of fairy splendor, Lindsay gives a clear statement of his idea that in film, the inanimate takes on a new life and often times becomes the dominate actor, embodying all of the elements of the characters which they represent. This anthropomorphic quality of the film is, Lindsay contends, one of its basic formative attributes. Furthermore, our visual culture has taught us to expect films to invest objects with life.

In the crowd pictures, the crowd becomes the dominate actor with the possibility of one or two persons within the crowd becoming representative of the entire mass. In such a case, the character assumes a universality which allows him to speak both for the immediate mass of which he is a part and for the nationality which he represents.

For an artistic corollary to the splendor genre, Lindsay turns to architecture. The basic connection between the splendor genre, and architecture would seem to lie in the fact that the splendor genre deals with objects or groups of people of epic proportions, while architecture as an art is also concerned with the pleasing and functional arrangement of masses. Thus Lindsay, when he refers to one of the splendor genres as an example of "architecture in motion" is speaking of the linear, textural, and spatial aspects of the film. Nevertheless, it would appear that the full significance of the concept of architecture in motion transcends a simple interest in line, texture, and space. Admittedly, Lindsay continues to express an interest in the pleasing pictorial arrangement, but his thoughts seem to go beyond an interest in a kind of "art for art's sake" photography. When compared with sculpture and painting in motion, architecture in motion appears to be a construct more oriented toward the symbolic function of film. In other words, there seems to be contained in the concept of architecture in motion, an interest in pictorial beauty <u>plus</u> an interest in pictures which carry

the <u>meaning</u> units of the film. This is borne out by the fact that

Lindsay devotes a large part of his discussion to an outline of the

anthropomorphic propensity of the film, and to an outline of the

symbolic or universal film character.

Throughout his analysis of the concept of architecture in motion

we can see that Lindsay's background in art is being used as the over-

all governing principle. Specifically, however, his very strong belief

in symbolic expression in art appears to exert greater influence on

architecture than on either sculpture or painting in motion.

NOTES

[1] Lindsay, The Art. . . , p. 30.

[2] Ibid., p. 31.

[3] It is interesting to note the striking similarity between this idea and Sergei Eisenstein's suggestion that the Japanese tanka is probably better understood if "represented visually." See Sergei Eisenstein, Film Form, trans. Jay Leyda (New York: Meridian Books, Inc., 1949), pp. 25-26.

[4] Lindsay, The Art. . . , p. 34.

[5] Ibid., p. 35.

[6] Ibid., p. 114.

[7] Ibid.

[8] Ibid., p. 119.

[9] Ibid.

[10] Ibid., p. 127.

[11] Ibid., pp. 127-128.

[12] Lindsay, "The Greatest. . . ," Barrett Collection, p. 203.

[13] Ibid., p. 170.

[14] Ibid., pp. 18-19.

[15] Lindsay, The Art. . . , p. 1

[16] Ibid., p. 54.

[17] Lindsay, "The Greatest. . . , "Barrett Collection, p. 69.

[18] Lindsay, "Poems Games for all the World," The Vitaphone, Barrett Collection, p. 5.

[19]Lindsay, The Art. . . , p. 39.

[20]Ibid., p. 40.

[21]Ibid., p. 43.

[22]Ibid., p. 46.

[23]Ibid., p. 51.

[24]Ibid., p. 62.

[25]Ibid., pp. 65-66.

[26]Ibid., p.66.

[27]Ibid., p. 67.

[28]Ibid., p. 68.

[29]Ibid., p. 69.

[30]Ibid., p. 70.

[31]Ibid., p. 73.

[32]Ibid., p. 75.

[33]Ibid.

[34]Ibid., pp. 77-78.

[35]Ibid., p. 133.

[36]Ibid., p. 134.

[37]Ibid., p. 135.

[38]Ibid.

[39]Ibid., p. 137.

[40] Ibid., p. 138.

[41] Ibid.

[42] Ibid., p. 139.

[43] Ibid., pp. 247-248.

[44] Lindsay, "Why I Think. . . ," Barrett Collection, pp. 9-10.

130

CHAPTER VIII

Hieroglyphics

I have read this chapter to a pretty neighbor who has approved of
the preceding portions of the book, whose mind, therefore, I
cannot but respect. My neighbor classes this discussion of
hieroglyphics as a fanciful flight rather than a sober argument.
I submit the verdict, then struggle against it while you read.[1]

Thus does Lindsay open his chapter on the hieroglyphics concept. It is

fair to say that he meets his neighbor's challenge, but loses the

struggle--at least in The Art of the Moving Picture. For although the

chapter entitled "hieroglyphics" contains a wealth of examples, it offers

nothing in the way of a precise definition of the term. The bulk of the

chapter is taken up with Lindsay's own reproductions of the ancient

Egyptian hieroglyphics, each of which is accompanied by his own inter-

pretation. And, in the sense that some of Lindsay's own personal inter-

pretations defy explanation, the chapter could rightfully be considered

a "fanciful flight." However, regardless of what Lindsay's pretty

neighbor might have thought of the chapter, or how mystical the chapter

may appear to the present-day reader, the concept of hieroglyphics was

important to Lindsay. The hieroglyphic idea is one which can be en-

countered throughout all of his writing. Unfortunately for the modern

reader, it is an idea which Lindsay never clearly defines. The nearest

he comes to a real definition of the idea is in the preface to his

Collected Poems:

I believe in a change in the actual fabric, not a vague new outline.
Therefore I begin with the hieroglyphic, the minute single cell of
our thought, the very definite alphabet with which we are to spell
out the first sentence of our great new vision. And I say: change
not the mass but change the fabric of your own soul and your own
visions, and you change all.[2]

Implicit here, is the beginning of a new form of visual symbolization
and communication. In other words, the hieroglyphic, to Lindsay's way
of thinking, is the beginning of a new visual alphabet which will enable
man to express his own highest visions and to comprehend those of others.
The specifics of this hieroglyphic method and its relation to film will
follow, but for the moment, let us outline some of the factors which
account for Lindsay's interest in the hieroglyphic idea.

Basic to any discussion of the hieroglyphic concept, is the knowledge that throughout his life, Lindsay was very much concerned with, to
use a clinical term, "externalizing" his innermost thoughts and aspira-
tions. This process of "externalizing" could take almost any form,
but in general the process meant making some sort of visual representation of one's inner thoughts--be it a picture, an hieroglyph, or a
poem. For instance, Lindsay himself often said that all of his poems
were preceded by a picture. No doubt such pictures were often pictures
in Lindsay's head, although there is some evidence to indicate that his
statement can be taken literally.[3]

It should also be noted that Lindsay's desire to make some sort of
tangible external representation of his inner feelings, did not always
turn toward straightforward, representational expression. In other
words, Lindsay felt compelled to express himself in symbolic fashion.
Apparently this was just a part of his make up, for as one friend put
it,

> His mind was filled with a complete world of symbols. They were
> personal but very real to him. When he said one of those mystify-
> ing things, it was a part of this very clear world of fantasy. . . .
> He had his own special pantheism, actively inhabited by symbol
> figures. He disdained translating these.[4]

Edgar Lee Masters, Lindsay's friend and biographer. tells us that Lind-

say exhibited a genius for seeing "symbols and meanings back of the real

and the apparent"[5] much in the same way the Blake and Swedenborg saw

them. Masters, however, is quick to point out that Lindsay's symbols

are entirely unique and not derived from either Blake or Swedenborg. As

was suggested earlier, Lindsay's symbolism was not restircted to his

literary efforts, but oftentimes took the form of pictures, many of

which were called hieroglyphics. Masters offers the following expla-

nation for Lindsay's hieroglyphics:

> Lindsay's eye, which was really lacking in penetration in many
> particulars, as for faces for example, and for reading men as men,
> was not helped by the welter of confusion which was about him in
> Springfield and America. He could well say that the American mind
> had become an overgrown forest of unorganized pictures, and that
> the whole world showed a like state by its grotesque and unsynthe-
> sized political cartooning. It was natural therefore, that he
> wanted to fetch forth the essential nature of the American mind,
> of Springfield, of many things by hieroglyphics which would settle
> his vision as to their nature, while it fixed their character in
> an art form.[6]

Worthy of note here are two important facts which help explain some of

Lindsay's highly personal hieroglyphics. First, they are very per-

sonal expressions which, as Masters suggests, help "settle" Lindsay's

own personal vision; they are, in a sense, a form of personal therapy.

And second, it should be noted that Lindsay's desire is to put his own

inner feelings into some sort of art form, usually symbolic. Such

highly personal symbolism then, may help explain many of the mystical

drawings which accompany Lindsay's poems.

Although Lindsay's highly personal form of symbolism may strike us

as entirely too personal and thus somewhat abstract, it is interesting

to note that his intention was the opposite. The following excerpt from a personal note book is of sufficient importance to present the discus-

ion to quote at length:

> Why not evolve the final pictures of the abstract and invisible
> things? Not by obscure symbolism, but by methods as direct and
> obvious as the soul of the spider and the soul of the butterfly.
> Let them set the pace for many more. . . . Now that we have be-
> gun to think, let every thought be as well carried as a rose
> petal, and as able to be pictured. Let us evolve a spiritual
> hieroglyphic, a heavenly sign language. Let the fiber of every
> dreaming picture be thought, thought, thought; let meaningless
> beauty be driven from the earth. Every heavenly thought has an
> earthly association or analogy; it should refer by suggestion,
> back to something seen before--greed should have a clutch to it,
> generosity should be lavish as a blowing rose, let it not be greed,
> but the soul of the greedy cut worm. It should not be generosity
> but the soul of the generous rose. It should be as close to
> pictures as pure decoration desires to get. The soul of the proud
> Bumblebee could come only after considerable study of that animal.
> Yet it should be free from all pictorial restraints. I have
> sufficient resources as a designer to carry out these. And the
> luxury of experiment needs a curb. It must not be an eternal
> habit going no further. I must put some order into the designs
> and I must reject even the borders that do not carry some weight
> of significance. It is well enough for other men's designs to be
> meaningless, but mine must be the servants of thought, of the
> thinking imagination. If the verses have borders, they should
> signify the verse meaning.7

Thus we can see that Lindsay's idea of symbolism was anything but

occult or abstract. Rather, it is apparent that the real essence of

visual expression is thought--thought which may be made visible. No-

where in this statement can one find evidence of a kind of art for art's

sake beauty. As Lindsay says, all beauty must have meaning--meaning

which arises from an external manifestation of some inner thought. Such

was a consuming passion with Lindsay throughout life.

Thus far, we have concentrated our attention only on the fact that

Lindsay was very much taken with the idea of symbolizing his innermost

thoughts. As yet, however, no attention has been given to the specific

method, or the hieroglyphic. There can be little doubt that hieroglyphic was simply Lindsay's word for symbol. The best evidence that the words symbol and hieroglyphic are one in the same lies in the fact that Lindsay, either consciously or unconsciously, uses the two interchangeably throughout his discussion of the hieroglyphic concept in The Art of the Moving Picture. Hieroglyphic is a word which Lindsay applies to any symbol, not just the symbolic process of the film. For instance, he sees the baseball bat and the cigar store Indian as typical "American hieroglyphics."[8] So, in reality, there is nothing peculiar or unique about Lindsay's idea of symbolism aside from the fact that he has given it a name which he feels is particularly apt. The choice of the word hieroglyphic apparently grew out of Lindsay's lifetime interest in the study of Egyptology. Lindsay's personal papers indicate that his library contained books in the subject and his personal notes and diaries are filled with sketches of the Egyptian hieroglyphic characters. As a result, in later life, Lindsay became quite proficient in duplicating the original Egyptian figures. Interestingly enough, however, it appears that his interest in Egyptian picture writing was limited, primarily, to the visual representations of thought which they presented to him. One researcher has confirmed the fact that Lindsay's actual knowledge of the Egyptian meaning of the hieroglyphics was sketchy.[9] Thus it can be said that Lindsay's use of and interest in hieroglyphics stems not from the fact that he was an astute Egyptologist, but rather from his desire to capitalize upon the Egyptians' highly visual form of communication. He was interested in a pictorial representation of thought. He had no interest in duplicating the language of the Egyptians, only an interest in employing their method.

In the final analysis his interest was not scholarly; it was aesthetic, and perhaps romantic.

Although it has been established that Lindsay's interest in the hieroglyphic idea was one which came from long association with Egyptology in general, Lindsay himself attributes his interest in the hieroglyphic to the movies. In a letter to a fellow poet, Lindsay says:

> The reason I am so mad over hieroglyphics is simply that I am movie saturated. . . . Such movie training is a suprising initiation into the whole Egyptian psychology of hieroglyphics. They had the most intense pictorial minds of any human beings who ever lived, and breathed, not excepting the Japanese, and right now I an nearer at home with a page of the Book of the Dead than I am with a page of Mr. Shakespeare or Marlowe.[10]

It may well be that the film heightened Lindsay's interest in the hieroglyphic as a symbolic form, yet the term hieroglyphic and its use as a synonym for symbol was a part of Lindsay's vocabulary and thought throughout his life.

Let us now turn to an examination of the term hieroglyphic as it is applied to the symbolic processes of film. Earlier it was noted that the hieroglyphic concept is never clearly defined in The Art of the Moving Picture. Thus the best way to get at precisely what Lindsay means by the term, is to look closely at some of the more elaborate examples of hieroglyphics which can be found in a review of A Romance of the Redwoods, a Cecil B. DeMille production starring Mary Pickford. The analysis of this particular film is based almost exclusively on the hieroglyphic concept.

The story concerns Jenny Lawrence, a yound New England orphan who is to be sent to her Uncle in California. As she packs for her journey, a tiny derringer is seen being hidden in her shoe. This, according to

Lindsay, is one of the major hieroglyphics of the film, and symbolizes,

"The spirit of Jenny."[11] Her uncle, who started his journey to Califor-

nia two months earlier, has been killed enroute by an Indian ambush,

and his identity, including name, clothing and papers, is taken on by a

fugitive, Black Brown. After a visit to a gambling hall with Brown,

the impostor, Jenny is given a true taste of the west. At this point,

Lindsay catalogues the following hieroglyphics: the arrow hole in her

true uncle's bloody papers, a black snake whip, Jenny's derringer,

Brown's six shooter, gambling paraphernalia, the silk hat of the boss

gambler, and dancing shadows on the doorways.[12] Jenny takes up

residence with Brown, and as she is doing his mending, she finds a

handkerchief mask, the next major hieroglyphic of the film--this one, of

course, being Brown's own personal hieroglyphic. The third outstanding

hieroglyphic of the story is a doll which Brown buys for Jenny. This,

Lindsay characterizes as a "humorous allusion to her size, but actually

the symbol of his tenderness for her."[13] Later, Jenny and Brown have

an argument in what Lindsay calls "sign conversation" in which the doll

is played against the mask and a letter which reveals the fact that

Brown has robbed and killed Dick Roland, and incidental character who has

befriended Jenny. Brown, attempting to repent, begins the ligitimate

pursuit of "washing gold." While he washes gold, Jenny washes clothes,

thus introducing another hieroglyphic. In Lindsay's eyes, the bundles

of laundry become hieroglyphics for "loyalty, taunting and embarrass-

ment."[14] Finally, an intricate plot is resolved as Jenny confesses she

is not Brown's niece, but his sweetheart. She then marries a reformed

Brown.

It is obvious, from examining these particular hieroglyphics, that Lindsay is speaking of visual cues which can be likened to what we would call symbols. Just how well such things as a derringer, a mask, and a doll measure up as "minute single cells of thought" would, it seems, depend upon how well they are developed within the film itself. Lindsay feels that one of the best ways to establish such a hieroglyphic or visual symbol is through repetition.[15] Apart from these considerations, it is quite apparent that hieroglyphics are, for the most part, objects which, through an early association which a character, become representative of that character or representative of his feelings. Thus we return to the connection between hieroglyphics and anthropomorphism, an idea which was developed in some detail in Chapter VII.

It is Lindsay's contention that hieroglyphics such as those discussed above, are, and should be, invested with a sense of life or with the qualities of the persons they represent. He says, for instance, that one of the reasons why the so-called colossal productions fail is because the movie audience has been taught to expect "conversations" between hieroglyphics of the type we have just discussed. It is his belief that one of the basic formative principles of the film is its ability to make the most microscopic object the dominant actor. In other words, sensible use of the close-up can transform small, inanimate objects into highly communicative hieroglyphics. Such is one of the reasons for the success of The Thief of Bagdad:

> It is one of the triumphs of The Thief of Bagdad that from first
> to last, every scene that is a principle scene, has for its central
> actor what would be a minute and inanimate thing upon the stage,
> and pretty generally an inanimate and ineffective symbol in fiction
> or verse.[16]

In addition, film also has the unique ability to take what Lindsay calls

the "giant hieroglyphic" and make it almost microscopic. In other words,

the extreme long shot which reduces things of epic proportions to mere

specks upon the horizon, can also serve as an hieroglyphic comment. Of

these two formative devices, the extreme long shot and the close-up, it

is Lindsay's contention that the latter is "certainly the most impor-

tant."[17] In the following we can see not only the importance of the

formative technique itself, but also the close relationship between the

concepts of hieroglyphics and anthropomorphism:

> When the Thief must hurry away, he carries with him, not the jewels
> which he had dreams of taking, but the beautiful slipper of the
> very beautiful princess. When he joins his satanic companion below
> the wall, he displays this slipper as a symbol of his change of
> heart. Now with many words in a novel, or with many gestures on
> the stage, such a slipper could be made into a symbol. In the story
> of Cinderella, by long repetition and by many devices, the glass
> slipper at last becomes a symbol of the love of man for woman and
> the fact that she has her foot upon his neck. It remains for the
> new art of the moving picture to take such a glittering thing, to
> show first its natural size, as one might say, under the microscope;
> then magnified till it fills the whole screen, then for the Thief
> to carry it from scene to scene, between the walls of the mystical
> City of Bagdad, where, as it looms large in his heart and imagina-
> tion, so it·looms large upon the screen, and just as the spectator
> might hold it to his own eye till it filled the whole horizon,
> likewise it seems to fill the whole life of this Thief. So his
> sudden change of heart is indicated with scarcely a title, and with
> no philosophizing or elaborations of words. Indeed, the thing tells
> its own story.[18]

Thus, because of the anthropomorphic quality of the film, we are able to

invest objects with a life which gives them symbolic meaning. It is

obvious from Lindsay's description of The Thief of Bagdad that he feels

film to be uniquely suited to the use of symbolic or hieroglyphic

objects. That is, as a result of formative techniques such as the long

shot and the close-up, film is able to establish inanimate objects as

symbols with far more economy of effort and far more force than either the stage or the novel.

With the exception of the "dancing shadows" which were listed as hieroglyphics of The Romance of the Redwoods, our discussion has been limited to hieroglyphic objects. However, Lindsay's use of the term extends much further. In addition to being applied to symbolic objects, hieroglyphic also can be a term which describes a symbolic action. For instance, Lindsay describes a scene from Griffith's The Avenging Conscience, in which a boy meditates upon a spider devouring a fly, and the spider, in turn, being destroyed by ants. Such microscopic action Lindsay sees as a particularly apt hieroglyphic because the action suggests to the boy, "how all nature stands on cruelty and the survival of the fittest."[19] Hieroglyphics or the hieroglyphic process can also be a way in which realistic setting and actions can be suggested through the use of the "near-Egyptian method."[20] In fact, there is some indication that Lindsay would actually prefer this type of production in that he states: "Photographic realism is splendidly put to route by powerful representation."[21]

Perhaps the most confusing facet of Lindsay's concept of hieroglyphic is his own personal interpretation of symbols. In The Art of the Moving Picture, in which Lindsay lists and describes several hieroglyphics based on the original Egyptian drawings, we find that his interpretation of the symbols is, in general, quite literal and traditional. In other words, the interpretation which he gives to various visual symbols is what one might expect from an unsophisticated observer. His interpretation of the noose may suffice as representative: "the noose may stand for solemn judgement and the hangman, it may also symbolize the snare of the fowler, temptation."[22] It would seem that

his interpretation of the noose as a symbol presents little that is

strikingly new or abstract in the way of symbolism, only a reiteration

of the traditional meaning which we give to objects. On the other hand

there are times when Lindsay sees things in his "hieroglyphs" which go

beyond the realm of credibility. Here is Lindsay's interpretation of

two objects in The Thief of Bagdad: "This [magic] crystal is a symbol

of wireless photography, just as the flying carpet is a symbol of modern

transportation and the flying machine."[23] It is not difficult to see the

difference between what Lindsay suggests as an interpretation of symbols,

and what he, personally, sees. He is obviously able to impart more far-

reaching meaning to these hieroglyphics than would be the average

viewer. Lindsay attempts, however, to present a rationale for his ex-

pansive interpretation of symbols. After listing and analyzing what he

considers to be the five major hieroglyphics of The Thief of Bagdad, he

admits that his reader might object to his "pouring into these five all

possible symbolism and history between here and the moon." He counters

this possible objection by saying:

> . . . remember we are establishing a new alphabet, or a very, very
> old one, and to resent the pouring of meaning into five hiero-
> glyphics is like resenting the use of the twenty-six letters of
> the alphabet, for upon the twenty-six letters of the alphabet the
> whole dictionary is based, and the endless combination of these
> twenty-six simplications make up English literature, and I would
> not be surprised if, in twenty years, we have our definite twenty-
> six or thirty established hieroglyphics in the motion picture
> field. . . .[24]

It is readily apparent that Lindsay sees his hieroglyphic system as the

beginning of a new alphabet with which we will be able to "spell out the

first sentence of our great new vision," the hope with which this

chapter began. Yet, it is equally apparent that Lindsay is either somewhat lacking in his knowledge of symbolism or is overly optimistic about
the power of symbols. Admittedly, Lindsay is prone to overstate his
case in an effort to make his point. This does not, however, justify
the dangerously weak analogy which he draws between his hieroglyphic and
the letters of the alphabet. There is no doubt that symbols are, and
always have been, a very basic and valuable technique of the cinema.
Nevertheless they cannot be compared with the unequivocal symbols of the
alphabet. Letters are invariant in meaning; symbols are not. Although
it is not made entirely clear in the above quote, it is conceivable that
Lindsay visualizes the hieroglyphic as similar to a letter in that only
when linked with another hieroglyphic does it assume meaning. If such
was his intention, then the analogy is a far more meaningful one. Still,
words, like symbols, are subject to multitudinous interpretations. It
is only when words and symbols are given a context that they lose at
least a part of their ambiguity. Perhaps the best explanation for Lindsay's visionary approach to the hieroglyphic concept is that in this
symbolic process, and for that matter throughout his writing on film,
he is seeking a means by which everyone may find in the film a modicum
of beauty and hidden meaning. Evidence of this can be found in The Art
of the Moving Picture:

> The more fastidious photoplay audience that uses the hieroglyphic
> hypothesis in analyzing the film before it, will acquire a new
> tolerance and understanding of the avalanche of photoplay con-
> ceptions, and find a promise of beauty in what have been properly
> classed as mediocre and sterotyped productions.[25]

Here we find an unqualified admission of the shortcomings of the film,
yet still present is a kind of blind acceptance of even the admittedly

mediocre film; an acceptance brought about by a consuming desire to find
the slightest "promise" of beauty. It is quite possible that Lindsay
is kinder to the films, or at least has more faith in them, than they
deserve. He appears to imbue them with his own evangelistic and
symbolic spirit. The lesson seems to be: have faith, and find your
own personal symbolic meaning and beauty. This lesson is an extension
of Lindsay's ideas as discussed in Chapters III and IV--his evangelistic
faith in the redemptive power of art and in individuality of expression.

In summary, we can see that, much like Lindsay's genre classifications of intimacy, action, and splendor, the term hieroglyphic loses its
potency as a precisely descriptive term, because of its diverse application. That is, hieroglyphic is not a symbolic process which applies
only to the film, or to pictorial symbolism alone. Rather, the hieroglyphic process appears to refer to any indirect or symbolic method of
expression, be it a picture, a poem, or whatever. The sole determinant
seems to be that whatever the means of symbolization, it must be an external manifestation of some inner thought, rather than feeling.

In function, the word hieroglyphic is most often applied to the
formative process whereby inanimate objects, because of continued
association with a particular character or action of the film, and because they are strengthened and made even more forceful by means of the
close-up, become symbolic of the character with whom they are associated.
Furthermore, Lindsay contends that this repetition and visual reinforce-
ment tend to invest objects with a life-like quality, thus inextricably
linking the hieroglyphic concept with his idea of anthropomorphism.

It becomes apparent too, that Lindsay sees in the hieroglyphic process, the beginnings of an entirely symbolic system of communication

in the film; a hope which no doubt derives from his own overwhelming

desire to symbolize, externally, all his own thoughts. Evidence of

his wish to apply this system to the film can be found in the following:

"I do not insist that the prospective author-producer adopt the hiero-

glyphic method as a routine, if he but consents in his meditative hours

to the point of view that it implies."[26] Lindsay seems to be asking

for a film which simply means something; a film which has a hidden

implication contained in the obvious; something which, because of this

indirect, symbolic expression, will lead the viewer toward some small

measure of speculative thought which will allow him to find that one

single symbolic expression of his own innermost thoughts.

NOTES

[1] Lindsay, The Art. . . , p. 171.

[2] Lindsay, Collected Poems, p. xxvi.

[3] Dura B. Cockerell, "Vachel Lindsay, Artist," manuscript, Lindsay-Cockerell Collection, Illinois State Historical Library, Springfield, n.d., p. 3. Mrs. Cockerell says: "Lindsay made the statement that every poem he ever wrote was first a picture, and in going over his sketches and manuscripts after his death this was found to be literally true."

[4] Letter from Isadora Bennett Reed, Lindsay collection, Lincoln Library, Springfield, Illinois, quoted in Kuykendall, "The Reading. . .", p. 71.

[5] Letter from Edgar Lee Masters, November 8, 1925, Barrett Collection.

[6] Masters, Vachel Lindsay. . . , pp. 272-273.

[7] Lindsay, Collected Poems, p. 366.

[8] From a personal diary, May 6, 1922, Barrett Collection.

[9] Heffernan, "The Ideas. . .," p. 42.

[10] Letter to John Drinkwater, February 16, 1925, Barrett Collection.

[11] Lindsay, New Republic, 11, p. 280.

[12] Ibid., p. 281.

[13] Ibid.

[14] Ibid.

[15] Lindsay, The Art. . . , p. 154.

[16] Lindsay, "The Greatest. . .," Barrett Collection, pp. 17-18.

[17] Ibid., p. 15.

[18]Ibid., p. 20.

[19]Lindsay, The Art. . . , pp. 124-125.

[20]Ibid., p. 237.

[21]Ibid.

[22]Ibid., p. 180.

[23]Lindsay, "The Greatest. . . ," Barrett Collection, p. 28.

[24]Ibid., p. 95.

[25]Lindsay, The Art. . . , p. 181.

[26]Ibid.

CHAPTER IX

Discussion

The purpose of this chapter is twofold. First the two sections
of the study will be drawn together in order to point up the relationship among Lindsay's views on art, poetry, religion, and society. Also
the chapter will discuss how this relationship shapes Lindsay's film
theory. Second, the totality of the study will be placed in the context
of the time. Particular attention will be paid to the way in which Lindsay's social views correspond with those of his contemporaries in art
and literature. Finally, Lindsay's film theory will be discussed in the
context of other theories.

Aside from the obvious influence of his art background there is
little evidence to suggest that Lindsay's views on religion and the
social milieu had any discernible direct effect on his structural theories. That is, it is difficult to see that Lindsay's strong religious
views were at work as he went about breaking the film into examples of
sculpture, painting, or architecture in motion. The point is, when one
separates Lindsay's structural theories from their mystical and evan-
gelical matrix, it becomes easier to see that he was simply a theorist
intent on sharpening his analytical tools. There are times when Lindsay
appears to lose his grip on these tools, yet he usually regains his
composure, and builds a new case for his original contention. Given
sufficient time, Lindsay will always retreat from his initial overstatement, and return to a more reasonable position.

Lindsay was enough of a graphic artist to want to know how the film
worked as a structural entity. And in a very real sense, his background

in art explains his neat, but sometimes unworkable, division of the film
into sculpture, painting, and architecture in motion. This approach is
nothing more or nothing less, than an example of a man who was working
with the theoretical and critical tools available to him and closest to
him. He has deep roots in the traditional arts, hence he uses them as a
basis structural foundation for this theory. In his approach, which
could be called one-sided, or even biased, Lindsay's theory is like
those of his contemporaries. Victor O. Freeburg's theory contains strong
overtones of a musical bias; Hugo Munsterberg writes from the viewpoint
of a clinical psychologist. So too have later theorists approached the
film with their own particular biases. Rudolph Arnheim's theory is a
Gestalt analysis of the way film functions. Much of what Bela Belazs
says in his theory is ultimately related to the mechanics of improving
the state by improving man's understanding of himself. Sergei Eisenstein
brings to his film theory a stage background and a fondness for a literary and rhetorical approach to the film. And Siegfried Kracauer's
theory is tainted by an unrequited love for physical reality. So Lindsay's theory is certainly not unique because of its personal bias; nor
can he be blamed for his exclusive emphasis upon the traditional arts
as standards of comparison. Like his contemporaries, and like those
who have followed him, he was working with what he knew best, the
graphic and plastic arts.

   Accepting Lindsay's theory for what it is, one grounded upon the
graphic and plastic arts, one must admit that his analogies from the
traditional arts are reasonably sound. At least the use to which he puts
them is unassailable. If one chooses to speak of the virtual depth of

the film it can be done only by comparing it with a traditional art form which uses the third dimension. Hence sculpture is the logical choice because it uses actual rather than virtual depth. The only other avenue available would be architecture which Lindsay sensibly reserves for a discussion of the monumental arrangements of people, buildings, and nature, which film often encompasses.

In the case of architecture, Lindsay had foresight enough to see that film had the capability of dealing with actions and objects of monumental proportions. He held that film exceeded the traditional arts in its ability to encompass that which is monumental in proportion and in its ability to reproduce gross actions and objects. Traditional art had attempted the same sort of epic portrayals in its mural painting, and this Lindsay realized. But, and this is the vital point, he also realized that film could surpass the art of mural painting by visual-izing the "mural" scene with motion. Another factor which placed film above mural painting was its ability to take liberties with the elements of time and space without destroying the logic of the visualization. Lindsay realized that much of mural painting was narrative in intent, that it attempted to tell "one picture stories." Yet mural painting could never quite do what film could. It could never deal discursively with time and space.

Concerning painting in motion, Lindsay recognized painting for what it was--a two dimensional medium which, by means of perspective, attempts to create the illusion of depth. But in the final analysis painting is a medium which can only work with what lies on the picture plane itself. Painting then becomes a meaningful artistic corollary for Lindsay's

discussion of those formative elements of the film which go to make up
the compositional elements of the picture plane. Just as had the
traditional artist before him, Lindsay realized that a part of the
beauty of the film could come from pleasing arrangements on a flat
surface. He understood that there were times when the thing being photographed did not demand a preoccupation with the illusion of depth, but
rather required an emphasis on the more subtle aspects of composition
such as tonal variations and the arrangements of figures within the
frame.

Lindsay's concept of anthropomorphism is dealt with under the
general heading of architecture in motion and under the specific heading
of furniture, trappings and inventions in motion. This is a particularly
appropriate categorization in that those objects which Lindsay describes
as being imbued with life, can be placed very neatly under the heading of
furniture, trappings, or inventions. Lindsay recognizes with considerable clarity the fact that film is capable of strengthening the relationship between people and objects by means of its formal structure. That
is, by using the closeup, film can simply make objects more forceful by
photographing them full frame and by continued repetition. Hence the
association of objects with people is easier in film than in the theatre
for instance. Anthropomorphism is, at its core, a symbolic process
whereby one thing stands for another.

There can be little doubt that Lindsay's idea of objects as actors
and his concept of hieroglyphics are one in the same. In both cases he
is speaking of the symbolic process of the film. If there is a difference between the two concepts it lies in the fact that when Lindsay

speaks of objects as actors he tends to use the word objects literally--
at least it appears to refer always to material objects, natural or man-
made. Hieroglyphics, on the other hand, can refer to more than objects.
For instance, a particular action can be an hieroglyphic and in some
cases Lindsay simply refers to pictures as hieroglyphs. Although anthropomorphism and hieroglyphics may differ in degree, they do not differ in
kind; both are symbolic processes. The degree to which they differ lies
in the fact that hieroglyphics is a general method for externalizing all
inner thought. It is not a process limited to use in the film. And
perhaps even more important, the idea of hieroglyphics goes much deeper
into the fabric of Lindsay's thought. It stems from his own personal
obsession to give outward meaning to his innermost thoughts. Hence
hieroglyphics is a more pervasive idea than anthropomorphism because it
is simply Lindsay's unbridled mysticism at work. The idea appears in all
his work, thus we can expect it to appear in his film work. It is inseparable from the Lindsay mentality.

   While it may be true that Lindsay sought refuge in his "hieroglyphic
mysticism,"[1] it was, nevertheless, a refuge which he sought very early
in life and one which he never left. To Lindsay's way of thinking
hieroglyphics, or at least the principle behind it, was the portent of
a whole new visual culture:

   We are now entering a new world that is a very old one. We are
   now closer to the Egyptian than to the Anglo Saxon civilization.
   I have taken many a young movie fan through the twelve magnificent rooms of the Egyptian section of the metropolitan museum.
   Always they are interested. Instantly they apprehend those
   marching hieroglyphics, those stone movies, upon the walls of the
   many reconstructed tombs in that magnificent gallery. They are
   sensitive to them in a way not comparable to their interest in the
   rest of the metropolitian.[2]

Lindsay's theoretical constructs, sculpture, painting, and architecture in motion, and their sometimes presumptuous application to the
traditional arts--to such classics as the Winged Victory and the Venus
De Milo--could very well be nothing more than an unconscious attempt to
give an element of respectability and sophistication to this new art.
He admitted that the film of his day was adolescent, yet he saw in it
what he wanted--some encouraging similarities to the established arts
with which he was so familar.

Although he never states it directly, Lindsay appears to look upon
film as a synthesis of the trends and forms of past art. This is not to
say that Lindsay believes film to be nothing more than a composite of
the traditional arts. Rather, he recognizes that the film draws on all
past arts, but in turn must adapt them to fit the peculiarities of the
new medium. In his writings he admits that novels, plays, and short
stories have made excellent motion pictures, but only after they have
been completely overhauled to fit the form of the new medium. Lindsay
knows that film and the traditional arts are compatible and that the
former owes much to the latter. But he realizes only too clearly that
each medium has its own means of expression: "A list of words making a
poem and a set of apparently equivalent pictures forming a photoplay may
have an entirely different outcome. It may be like trying to see a per-
fume or listen to a taste."[3]

Beyond the similarities which Lindsay saw between the traditional
arts and the film, he also noted some differences which, in his esti-
mation, placed film above the older arts in its ability to visualize
ideas. Film could manipulate time and space, vitalize objects, depict

continuous movement in pictorial form, encompass scenes of epic proportions, and exercise its powers of symbolization, particularly in the
area of continued association so necessary for effective symbolism.
These were the formative capabilities which Lindsay extracted; these
were the fruits of his analysis, and it was because of them that he saw
a bright future for the film as an art of visualization.

It has been this writer's position that Lindsay's views on religion
and the social milieu are not directly operative in his structural
analysis of the film; in the way he disects the film and views its form.
Such a position is not, of course, a radical one, in that the formal
techniques of film are devoid of any such human predispositions; the
formal techniques of film exist as neutral elements. However, the way
these elements are put together and the purpose for which they are
assembled can be influenced by human predispositions. In much the same
way, Lindsay's structural analysis is influenced, or perhaps motivated
by his predilections. In other words, the use to which he would put the
formal techniques which he isolated largely is determined by his views
on religion, aesthetics, and the social milieu. This accounts for the
fact that a large part of The Art of the Moving Picture is devoted to a
social thoery of film. In other words, after Lindsay thoroughly has
analyzed the formal structure of the film, he then takes the result of
his analysis and gives it a social function. As he would have it, we
should "put the art thought of the world in motion instead of the entire
decorative instinct of our more expensive department stores."[4] Or put
another way, Lindsay is interested in freeing the formative elements of
the film from their mechanical fetters:

The first reason for making motion pictures that have the qualities
of good painting is that this is the main chance to overcome the
machine-like effects of the photoplays. Mechanical pictures are
unpleasant pictures.5

Thus far, we have seen that Lindsay's background in art had an

obvious influence on his structural analysis of the film both in the

method he used, and as a motivation for the analysis itself. Further-

more, it has been suggested that Lindsay's religious and social views

played little, if any, part in his structural analysis. Rather, his

religious and social views become influential only when he begins to

apply his structural analysis to the overall function of film in society.

Let us turn now to an examination of the way in which Lindsay's religious

and social views seem to have influenced his thinking about the position

of film in society.

It must be understood that all of Lindsay's comments about the

social function of film are based upon the supposition that his own

analysis of the film is basically sound, and that film is, or is at

least capable of becoming, an art of beauty. It will be remembered

from Chapters III and IV that art and religion are mutually dependent,

and that in turn, both are dependent upon beauty. In Lindsay's

asethetic, there is no place for the ugly or grotesque. Hence, armed

with the knowledge that art must be beautiful, and that this beauty is

the revelation of God, we find that Lindsay visualizes film as an art

capable of conveying the spiritual message which he feels is so essential

to the well being of the country. The clearest and most complete ex-

pression of this idea comes near the end of The Art of the Moving

Picture:

Man will not only see visions again, but machines themselves, in
the hands of prophets, will see visions. In the hands of
commercial men they are seeing alleged visions, and the term
'vision' is a part of moving-picture studio slang, unutterably
cheapening religion and tradition. When Confucius came, he said
one of his tasks was the rectification of names. The leaders of
this age should see that this word 'vision' comes to mean something more than a piece of studio slang. If it is the conviction
of serious minds that the mass of men shall never again see
pictures out of Heaven except through such mediums as the kinetoscope lens, let all the higher forces of our land courageously lay
hold upon this thing that saves us from perpetual spiritual·
blindness.[6]

Not only is this statement an admonition to use the medium to its

fullest social potential, it is also the familiar plea for "artists"

who will exploit the formative potential of the film. It should be

stressed that when Lindsay uses such phraseology as "pictures out of

heaven" he is not necessarily speaking in a literal sense, but rather is

refering to his own ascending hierarchy of art, beauty, and religion.

In other words, according to Lindsay's lexicon, "pictures out of heaven"

could mean pictures of a secular nature which elicit the type of beauty

which he feels is a representative manifestation of the spiritual power

behind them. At any rate it is apparent that if film is to serve a pro-

ductive social function, it must be an art form whose final effect is

spiritually uplifting. Film becomes a synthesis of past forms and

present needs.

A specific tenet of Disciples theology which has an interesting

parallel in Lindsay's social plan for the film is the church's idea of

unification. It has been noted that one of the basic tenets, in fact

the reason for the existence of the Campbellite faith, is its desire to

unify all Christian faiths. In a similar fashion, Lindsay views the

film as an instrument which can bring people to a better understanding of each other, thus unifying them. Although Lindsay does not speak of

the unification idea in terms of bringing together individual religious

denominations, he does see the film as an instrument whereby man's

aesthetic sensibilities can be developed, thus making all men one in

spirit. And it is for this very reason that Lindsay has great hopes for

the film as the first truly democratic art. Only through democracy,

which Lindsay sees as a kind of socialistic, classless society, govern-

ed by mass taste, can man live in spiritual harmony. Perhaps the prime

reason for Lindsay's contention that the film offers the greatest

opportunity for spreading his democratic idea lies in the fact that film,

like the newspaper, reaches practically all of the population. As he

puts it, the film "goes almost as far as journalism into the social

fabric in some ways, further in others."[7] In fact, Lindsay likens the

invention of the film to the invention of the press. He says: "Edison

is the new Gutenberg. He has invented the new printing. The state that

realizes this may lead the soul of America, day after tomorrow."[8] Film

then, like printing, is truly a mass medium which can make more know-

ledge and more art available to more people. Unlike printing, however,

the film does not demand a prerequisite literacy because it is a means

of communication which works through the visual channel alone.[9] Thus,

film is a genuinely democratic art because it is available to all people,

regardless of station, regardless of education. Lindsay recognized the

basically "democratic" nature of the film as early as 1915, and in that

year wrote:

> I have the extraordinary sensation that I have in a way vindicated
> my long blind-alley gropings as an art student--and some of the
> vague generalizations in the Adventures While Preaching the Gospel

of Beauty. Here is that Democratic art of which I vaguely talked.10

Lindsay believes that as a natural result of film being a democratic art

which penetrates to the darkest, most remote corners of the country, it

is also, therefore, the art which is changing the very culture of the

country--even the way we think. In a word, he saw the film as a harbing-

er of a new visual culture.

Basic to an understanding of the idea of a new "visual culture,"

is the knowledge that Lindsay held to the firm conviction that "we

think in pictures if we think at all."[11] It must also be understood

that he did not necessarily attribute this visual thinking to the in-

fluence of the film, but merely insisted that the film was perpetuating

this type of visual conceptualization. He did hold that as long as the

film was contributing to the multitude of pictures which are changing

our culture, it was by far the best method of organizing and shaping our

visual culture. As might be expected of a poet, Lindsay expresses some

concern regarding this trend toward a pictorial society:

> We are sweeping into new times, in which the eye is invading the
> province of the ear, and in which pictures are crowding all
> literature to the wall, and if some of the dressed up steerage
> passengers had their way, they would crowd all history to the
> wall. We can view this tendency with mixed emotions. On the
> whole there is more joy than sorrow in the adventure.[12]

The obvious reservations which Lindsay has about this trend derive from

his belief that if allowed to continue undisciplined, the trend will

lead to a sort of visual chaos in which the country will have nothing

but an amorphous mass of meaningless pictures. And, as we have seen

throughout this study, meaningless pictures, as far as Lindsay is

concerned, are worthless pictures. The whole movement toward over-

visualization is leading, he believes, toward what Lindsay calls an

"hieroglyphic mood."[13] This hieroglyphic mood is one which can be seen
in the political cartooning of J.N. "Ding" Darling, and in the advertising which permeates much of the material that we read. Lindsay
suggests that if one will only look at the magazine stands he will quickly see how a magazine such as the Saturday Evening Post is "nothing but
a condensed billboard" whose advertising is "much closer to Egyptian
hieroglyphics than anything in the history of printing, good or bad."[14]
Even though advertising and cartooning may be approaching the Egyptian
hieroglyphics of which he was so fond, Lindsay still views the unbridled growth with some alarm, and calls it a "riot of hieroglyphics."[15]

Lindsay attributes the ever-increasing use of pictures as a means
of communication, to technological refinements which are making the
printing process far simpler and more economical. So simple is the
process that we have had cartoons "dumped" upon us until Andy Gump is
"more familiar than any character in mere literature."[16] As was noted
in Chapter II, Lindsay was not in sympathy with the technological
revolutions of his time, therefore it is tenable that he views the trend
with alarm simply because it is the result of the same technology of
which he was skeptical. At any rate, the ease with which the multitude
of pictures are turned out gives Lindsay pause because of the lack of
guidance in the production of these hieroglyphs. As he puts it,

> If we do not have some kind of continence and direction in this
> matter of speeded-up, unreasoning hieroglyphics, the brain of man
> becomes in this modern hour simply a circus gone wrong, a Ringling
> circus, a gigantic spectacle, but not set in order, not harmonized
> by a stage manager, with a sense of color, or form. . . .[17]

If these pictures are to be re-ordered, and if we are to be spared
visual catastrophe, it is Lindsay's belief that we must look to the

film for guidance.

To counteract the confusion which is fast arising from the proliferation of visual images, Lindsay suggests that we must look to the
film. He reasons as follows:

> This way of thinking from picture to picture, of leaping from
> vision, to vision, without sound, without gesture, without the
> use of English, with as little use of type as possible, this
> tendency increasing every hour, must be ruled by the motion
> picture, if it is to have any direction and leading, because
> the motion picture is so much more powerful than all the rest,
> by reason of the occult elements of motion and light.[18]

Although he attributes the power of the film to elements of "motion and

light," another way in which the film can bring order out of visual

chaos is by means of its ability to organize pictures into a meaningful,

syntactical structure. For example, Lindsay says that it is a credit to

The Thief of Bagdad that all of the pictures fall into place with

clarity and order. He says of the organization of the film:

> We step definitely from word to word, sentence to sentence,
> paragraph to paragraph, in a well-organized, new style of
> picture writing, as telling, as grammatical, and as artistic
> as any language organized upon the face of the Earth. It is
> colloquial, idiomatic, and of bounding vitality.[19]

Such a meaningful arrangement of pictures in the film has the effect of

moving the human mind along "irresistably," as Lindsay puts it.[20] But

in contrast to this syntactical arrangement of visual images is the

welter of confused and poorly conceived images of the new "hieroglyphic

mood"; a mood whose improvement is being forced upon it because man's

sense of what is worth seeing is becoming greatly improved.[21] As a

result of the influence of film, we have achieved a kind of pictorial

literacy which comes only with the proper eye training.[22]

It is tenable that a man who believes that the entire national

cultural fabric is being changed by an emphasis upon visual rather than
literary culture, is a man who would be vitally concerned with a theory
of film which attempts to analyze the formal aspects of the medium.
Hence we return to the thesis with which this discussion began: Lindsay's deep-seated interest in religion and the social milieu provides
the motivation for his structural analysis, but does not affect the
analysis itself.

While the tie is not immediately apparent, Lindsay's idea of a new
visual culture and his assessment of his own poetry are not too far
separated, in that as a poet, Lindsay believed himself to be a maker of
pictures; even as a poet, he was a contributor to the new visual culture. Lindsay preached and practiced his theories of art throughout
his life, even though he achieved fame and was recognized by most
people as a poet. Nevertheless, he was never quite at home with the
title of poet, for it was his feeling that he was, first and last, a
graphic artist rather than a verbal artist. As he says in his Collected
Poems,

> [The Art of the Moving Picture] champions my favorite notions of
> Painting, Sculpture, Architecture and Hieroglyphics. I have been
> an art student all my life, in the strictest sense of the word.
> I have been so exclusively an art student, I am still suprised
> to be called a writer.23

Not only does Lindsay look upon himself as an art student, but as an art
student-poet whose ideas on art are best expressed in a book about the
motion picture. Hopefully, the relationship among art, poetry, and
film will be clarified before this discussion ends.

Throughout the preface to his Collected Poems Lindsay chafes under
the criticism which has been leveled at his attempt to mix poetry and

pictures. At times, one senses that the whole undercurrent of the preface is a defense of his position as a maker of pictures. For instance,
very early in the preface, Lindsay asks his reader to pay particular
attention to the designs as he reads the poetry because, he insists, the
poems grew out of the designs.[24] If the ideas for his poems did not
come directly from designs, he says that many of them came from "pictures in the air"[25] which he has seen. So strong has been the influence of art upon his poetry that Lindsay finally issues a plea for
acceptance of his poetry as pictorial:

> My little world still insists I am a student of phonetics. But
> it seems to me reasonable that. . . my verse be judged not as a
> series of experiments in sound, but for a lifetime and even here-
> ditary thoughts and memories of painting. Let the verse be
> scrutinized for evidence of experience in drawing from life,
> drawing architecture, drawing sculpture, trying to draw the
> Venus of Milo, and imitating the Japanese Prints and Beardsley,
> and trying to draw like Blake, and all such matters.[26]

With the knowledge that Lindsay looked upon his poetry as "pictorially
inspired" it is easy to understand why he is sometimes classified as an
imagist poet. It seems only natural that his poetry would take this
course, and would be, as Wilkinson has suggested, "a series of related
images, presented in organic rhythm and suggesting a mood."[27] Yet for
all the images which Lindsay's poetry may conjure up in the mind, there
is no denying that his poetry depends very heavily upon rhythm for the
production of these images, rather than upon verbal imagery alone.
Nonetheless, if we can accept Lindsay's own assessment of what inspired
his poetry and the evaluation of critics, it safely can be said that
his poetry was both visually inspired and imagistic in its final effect.
Although Lindsay never calls himself an Imagist he sees a tie between
the so-called Imagist poetry and film. He says that the "Imagist

impulse need not be confined to verse," because there is a "clear
parallelism between their point of view in verse and the Intimate and
friendly photoplay."[28] If someone were to develop Imagist photoplays,
says Lindsay, they would be like Japanese prints and painting come to
life, "Pompeian mosaics in Kaleidoscopic but logical succession,
Beardsley drawings made into actors and scenery, [and] Greek vase-paint-
ing in motion."[29]

Knowing what we do of Lindsay's social conscience, it is not
surprising that the "pictures in his head" were put into poetic form for
a better reason than simply adding more pictures to the confusion of the
visual culture which he says was developing. His poetry was not simply
a matter of therapy through self-expression. Rather, like his film
theory, and like his ideas about the traditional arts, Lindsay's poetry
has behind it a social purpose which was infused with the democratic
ideal which is so prevalent in all of his thinking. It was his belief
that if poetry is to serve its true function, it must be an art which is
available to all people, even the unlettered. It should speak to
Americans about America, just as all arts should. This mass theory of
art explains the highly topical nature of his poetry, and in the
opinion of some critics it also explains the short life of Lindsay's
work.[30]

Lindsay's theory of poetry then, is similar to his theory of film
in that both are pictorially oriented, and both, by his own admission,
are the product of a man who would rather be remembered as an art
student. Naturally his fondness for the pictorial arts as such would be
more apparent in his film theory than in his ideas on poetry. Yet if

we can accept Lindsay's stated theories about his poetry, the same in-
fluences from the graphic and plastic arts were at work in his poetry.
It is of some significance too, that whenever Lindsay speaks of his
theory of pictorial poetry he refers his reader to The Art of the Moving
Picture for a more detailed development of his ideas.[31] This constant
cross-referencing between his poetry and his film book indicates the influence of the traditional arts on both his film and poetic theory and
thus establishes a clear relationship between the two. Not to be denied
either is the social purpose behind both his poetry and his film theory.
Of Adventure While Preaching the Gospel of Beauty, the work which outlines the social mission of his poetry, Lindsay says:

> It is not even a rhymer's book. It is an art-student's book, from
> first to last. I consider it the final test, the central point of
> my work. All these pictures [the visual inspiration for his
> poetry] are implied in it. Closely related to it [is] The Art of
> the Moving Picture.[32]

Again, Lindsay deliberately connects his poetry and film theory, this
time in terms of their social purpose. Of this we can be sure: The
intent of both his poetry and film theory was the same. Both should
work toward the betterment of the society in which they exist. As a
poet, Lindsay was a troubador who tramped about the country reciting his
own uniquely American verses. But in the film, he recognized a medium
which could preach his mass "Gospel of Beauty" on a much broader and a
much grander scale than any troubador could ever hope to do.

As an art theorist and a social critic, Lindsay was not as radical
as first he might appear. While his thoughts were couched in visionary
and sometimes incomprehensible terms, they were not widely divergent
from a strain of thinking which found expression in the work of other

artists and writers of the period. The difference between Lindsay and his contemporaries was, of course, in the means which they suggested for the improvement of the society. Lindsay looked to the film to solve the social ills, while his contemporaries looked to their own arts for a solution, or at least used their arts as a means of exposing what they believed to be evils. Regardless of the means which these men suggested --art, literature, or film--their end was similar.

We have seen, for instance, that Lindsay's insistence upon a thoroughly American art and his writing of what was undoubtedly some very topical American poetry, was but a continuation of the nationalistic spirit in art which began with Robert Henri, Lindsay's influential art teacher. Furthermore, Lindsay's Populist views, or his desire to re-turn to the agrarian simplicity of the early nineteenth century was a part of a strain of thinking which manifested itself in the work of Edgar Lee Masters and Carl Sandburg in poetry, and in the art of Thomas Hart Benton, John Curry and Grant Wood. It is of more than passing significance that the above-mentioned figures in literature and art were, for the most part, products of the midwest. Although he never bothers to define the quality, Lindsay was of the opinion that the midwest possessed a inspirational quality which was responsible for a number of literary works which were being published at the same time as his. He notes that in the same year his Golden Book of Springfield was publish-ed, Edgar Lee Masters' Mitch Miller and Doomesday Book were released, Sinclair Lewis' Main Street was popular, Floyd Dell's Moon Calf was being praised as a study of a midwestern town, and Sherwood Anderson wrote Poor White, another penetrating study of the midwest.[33] Of this

flurry of midwestern literature, Lindsay says: "One may agree that the
middle west is having its innings in much of the most honest, the least
tricky and commercial literary work of our immediate time."[34] Although
Lindsay contends that the midwest is a milieu which has nurtured considerable writing of some import, it should be noted that he is not in
complete agreement with some of these writers' criticism of the people
and mores of the midwest. In principle, he agrees with what many of
them are fighting for, but in terms of their specific criticism, he disagrees. For example, he says that Sinclair Lewis and H.L. Mencken are
"the two most valuable citizens right now, from the standpoint of free
speech, a free press and personal courage at all times."[35] But Lindsay
is quick to say that he disagrees with them both on the point of liberal
protestantism, which is "far more a source of life and light than these
two gentlemen will concede."[36]

As Masters suggests, Lindsay bears as much similarity to Walt
Whitman as to any other contemporary literary figure, but the similarity
is only in their boundless faith in America, and not in any creed of
life or writing. Whitman sounds most like Lindsay when he resolves to
"map-out, fashion, form and knit and sing the ideal American, to project
the future, and to depend on the future for an audience."[37] To see the
kinship between the basic beliefs of the two men, one need only look at
the final chapter of The Art of the Moving Picture in which Lindsay
admonishes the film maker who would do justice to his art, to "set before
the world a new group of pictures of the future" and to "show us every-
day America as it will be when we are only halfway to the millennium yet
thousands of years in the future."[38] Except for the fact that the two

men are speaking of different modes of expression--Whitman literature

and Lindsay film--their ideals could be exchanged in toto.

One element of Lindsay's personality, and therefore his writing,

which distinguishes him, at least in degree, from some of the figures

just discussed, is his evangelistic fervor. Lindsay did not often

simply say that something was wrong, but more often than not, he shouted

it. The same is true for what he felt to be right. The right too, was

shouted. Hence, he invariably tends to overstate his case. Much of the

evangelism and unbelievable prophecies of his film theory can be ex-

plained by his desire to emphasize his point in the only way that he

knew--through overstatement. Yet, Lindsay's evangelistic fervor was

not unique, because some of his contemporaries used the same approach.

In the art world, Rockwell Kent spoke loudly and forcefully about

his pet social theories, some of which could pass for Lindsay's. But

for the difference in style, the following excerpt from Kent's auto-

biography, could have been written by Lindsay:

> Hadn't we in the years of our lives read enough, thought enough,
> knocked about the world enough, and seen enough to have learned
> at least not to be taken into camp and shorn of common sense by
> that claque for urban life and values, that chamber of commerce
> of the urban arts, that strident, cheering, wooing, pleasing
> "come on in" of drowning Loreleis which plays the theme song of
> the cities' culture? "This is life," say the poor in their
> tenements; "This is life" say the big business men of Wall Street
> and the little businessmen of Third Avenue, say the fans at the
> Garden and the Opera, say couples in Riverside apartments and
> couples whispering in East Side vestibules. "It's the life," says
> the gangster, "Sure it's life," says the cop. Smoke, grime, noise
> bustle, packed sidewalks, jammed subways, choked traffic; noise of
> traffic horns, of jazz, of riveters. "Paint it" the critics cry.
> "Play it with instruments, carve it in stone, sing it in madrigals
> and odes and sonnets, write novels around it, treatises about it:
> act it, preach it, shout it, din it. Now all together, boys of
> the arts, press, stage, screen, platform: THIS IS AMERICA! Like
> hell it is. It is the city and no more. We have only to tour

America by plane, and from the little height of some thousands of
feet to which it carries us look down, to read in the all but endless and unbroken verdure of its countenance our land's true
character. Green countryside; meadows and pasturelands and cultivated fields; forests and wilderness; mile after mile for hours on
end the green, green land glides by. Houses? And settlements?
Of course. Like grains of salt spread sparsely on a table top.
And now and then--hours, perhaps, between--a murky streak, a smudge
of smoke far off: a city! One mile in area, in forty-seven
thousand miles of green. How foolish must the cities pride appear
to the all-seeing eyes of God.39

Equally vociferous in his criticism of the age was Louis Sullivan,

one of the most controversial and evangelistic figures in the history

of American architecture. Shortly after the turn of the century,

Sullivan began a series of polemic articles called Kindergarten Chats,

in which he deprecated both the architecture and the architects of the

day. In the vigor of his criticism Sullivan very much resembles Lind-

say in that both men accuse the so-called culture bearing class of

having little, if any, taste. Like Lindsay, Sullivan held that it is

the duty of the artist to represent the society in which he works, and

that what he does with that trust is a justifiable inquiry in a

democratic society. Furthermore, Sullivan expresses great faith in the

fundamental good sense of the masses and believes, just as did Lindsay,

that as a nation and as a people, we have the ability to appreciate

beauty and greatness.40 Last, and certainly not least of the similar-

ities between the social and artistic theories of the two men, is

Sullivan's plea for indigenous architecture. Speaking of the pseudo-

Roman architecture which prevailed in America, Sullivan says: "Roman

was Roman: American is, and is to be American. The Architect should

know this without our teaching, and I suspect that he does know it

very well in his unmercenary moments."41

As a social critic Lindsay is a part of the intellectural ferment
in art and literature which began shortly after the turn of the century.
His was a flamboyant and mystical voice which added to the discontent
which writers and artists of the time expressed regarding the changes
which were taking place within the country. Lindsay's criticism was less
caustic than some of his contemporaries, but without doubt he could match
any of them in the evangelistic fervor with which he suggested remedies
for what he considered to be the social problems of the day. Lindsay
differed with some of his fellow critics as to the effects of these
social changes. For instance, Lewis and Mencken were convinced that some
of the trends of the times were intellectually harmful, whereas Lindsay
objects to them on the grounds that they were leading to moral decay in
America. Lindsay was unique only in that he proposed the use of a new
and different art form, the film, as a means for improving society.
Film, because it was a synthesis of the traditional forms of art and
literature, was a far more powerful force for the betterment of society
than either literature or art as individual art forms. Now that we have
compared Lindsay with some of his contemporaries in literature and art,
let us turn to an examination of Lindsay as he relates to other film
theorists.

To say that Lindsay's theory as a whole resembles one particular
theorist more than another, would be inaccurate and dangerous. It would
be inaccurate because Lindsay was the first to theorize about the film,
therefore any comparison that is made must contain, somewhere, the
admission that other theorists resemble Lindsay. It would be dangerous
because the reader might feel a compulsion to infer that Lindsay's theory

had a direct influence on those who followed him. This writer is not
willing either to make or allow such an unwarranted inference. All one
safely can say about Lindsay's film theory and the theories that followed is that there are very definite similarities; similarities which
easily could be attributed to the fact that the formal structure of film
admits of only certain areas of theoretical considerations, thus all
theorists eventually end up talking about the same thing, only in
different terms. Therefore, the prime purpose of the discussion which
follows is to point up the similarities between the theories of Lindsay
and those who followed him, and the difference in intensity with which
each pursued his theoretical notions. No attempt will be made to make
a one to one comparison between Lindsay and all other theorists. All of
Lindsay's major theoretical constructs will be treated but they will be
compared only with the theorist whose ideas bear the most resemblance
to Lindsay's.

Pictorial beauty, a very serious consideration in Lindsay's theory,
receives as much attention as any other single concept in his entire
theory. But, as we have seen, his analysis is based on standards which
he transfers from the graphic arts, and it is this very transference
that hinders Lindsay's analysis of pictorial beauty. He uses the
graphic arts as a means for extracting and isolating the individual
formal elements of the film. Painting in motion is the concept in which
Lindsay treats the compositional elements of the picture plane itself.
Sculpture in motion is used to discuss the illusory character of the
film, or depth, and architecture in motion deals, primarily, with the
more complex meaning units of the film. Basically the method is sound,

but with one exception. Lindsay's categorization is too severe and does not allow for the relationship which exists among these three concepts. Undoubtedly Lindsay knows the relationship exists, but his own structured analysis avoids a blending of all these formative elements. Therefore, an integrated discussion of all the elements of pictorial beauty, is lacking. It is left to the reader to piece together the overall view.

The theorist who most resembles Lindsay in his devotion to pictorial beauty, is Victor O. Freeburg. In addition to an entire book dealing with pictorial composition in the film,[42] Freeburg devotes a large portion of The Art of Photoplay Making to a discussion of pictorial beauty. Sounding much like Lindsay, Freeburg insists that the primary appeal of the film is to the eye, and that the film can never impress the viewer pictorially, unless it produces beautiful pictures.[43] Freeburg sees a similarity between sculpture, painting and architecture and the pictorial aspects of the film. In fact he also suggests that the film maker may learn the basic principles of pictorial composition by studying the "masterpieces of centuries gone by."[44] For all their similarity in approach, the thing which differentiates Freeburg from Lindsay is the former's recognition of and detailed discussion of moving composition, the one element that clearly separated the traditional arts from the film. Lindsay too recognizes the element of movement, but has a tendency to discuss static composition and then superimpose movement over it, thus producing a sort of two-layered treatment of composition rather than an integrated discussion of movement and composition, as is the case with Freeburg.

Generally speaking, Freeburg's discussion of pictorial composition,

while it resembles Lindsay's, is far more sophisticated and far more
detailed. Clearly, it reveals an analytical sense which Lindsay seems
to lack. While Freeburg pursues static composition and moving composition to their ultimate conclusion, Lindsay seems to have only an immediate intuitive grasp of them which he never succeeds in rendering in his
work. Lindsay tends to expect a one to one carry-over from the graphic
and plastic arts to the film. Before leaving the subject of pictorial
composition as such, we should look at the illusionary aspect of composition or the element of depth.

Lindsay sees an analogy between the plastic and dimensional nature
of sculpture and the apparent depth of the three dimensional image re-
produced on a plane surface. He recognizes that the viewer imparts a
sense of depth to the photographic image, but stops with this simple
assertion. Hugo Munsterberg, writing just one year after the publication
of Lindsay's ideas, gives a very thorough, even clinical, analysis of
the illusion of depth in film. Yet for all its sophistication, Munsterberg's analysis starts with precisely the same analogy as Lindsay's--
sculpture and architecture. Aside from his psychological analysis of the
illusion of depth, the one thing which sets Munsterberg's analysis apart
from and above Lindsay's is Munsterberg's acute awareness of the importance of movement as a contributing factor in the illusion of depth.
Munsterberg maintains that the flatness of the motion picture screen is
a part of our objective knowledge, but that we _perceive_ depth in the
picture on the screen. Furthermore, our perception of depth is aided
because "we are there in the midst of a three-dimensional world, and the
movements of the persons or of the animals or even of the lifeless

things. . . strongly maintain our immediate impression of depth."[45] Not
to be denied is the possibility that Lindsay, in his insistence that the
action picture most often displays the illusion of depth, had the germ
of the idea which Munsterberg develops far more fully. Also, it should
be added that Munsterberg's background as an experimental psychologist
equipped him to produce a more penetrating analysis of depth, which is
after all, a psychological phenomenon.

Another pervasive element of Lindsay's film theory is his interest
in the symbolic process of the medium. As Lindsay's theory is arranged,
the symbolic character of the film is treated in his idea of the inanimate as actor and in his concept of hieroglyphics. Lindsay believes
that film has the ability to imbue objects with a sense of life and
vitality. He contends that because of the film's ability to enlarge
objects, to constantly repeat them, and to draw relationships between
them and people, objects become symbolic of the very people with whom
they are associated. Such an association or symbolic process, Lindsay
calls hieroglyphics. In Lindsay's lexicon, the hieroglyphic process is
a symbolic process which can be applied to any sort of communication
situation, and it not limited to use in the film. However, when he
applies the term hieroglyphic to a particular film, or event within a
film, he is normally speaking of a kind of symbolization which results
from either objects assuming the role of actors, or a kind of _pars pro_
toto. Undoubtedly the concept of _pars pro toto_ is indicative of Lindsay's desire to reduce all expression to one single "hieroglyphic" or
symbolic thought. And, it is this very desire which leads him to over-
estimate the power of the symbolic process in film. Lindsay's own

mysticism and his infatuation with the hieroglyphic process lead to a
highly subjective interpretation of symbols which, for the most part,
remains incomprehensible. Nonetheless, one is forced to admit that
Lindsay possesses a sound basic understanding of the symbolic function
of film.

Anyone who calls himself, or is called, a film theorist is likely
to discuss the symbolic character of the film because it is an integral
part of the formative process of the film. Among the theorists who
treat the symbolic process, two work from the same basic premise, yet
present discussions which are far more detailed than Lindsay's.
Although his discussion of symbolism lacks the mystical flights of fancy
that Lindsay's does, Victor O. Freeburg holds to the same basic notion
that because symbolism permeates all forms of expression, "it follows
that it should be mastered as a means of expression in the new art of
the photoplay."[46] Like Lindsay, Freeburg contends that film is particularly well adapted to the use of objects as symbols because of the
formative capabilities of the close-up. Both theorists contend that
because of the selectivity of the close-up, objects can be made forceful because of their visual prominence and thus the substitution of
object for actor or idea is more easily and meaningful established.
Certainly more sophisticated than either Lindsay or Freeburg's treatment of symbolism, is Sergei Eisenstein's discussion of the substitution
of objects for actors, or what he calls the concept of pars pro toto.
Eisenstein believes that the substitutions of the part for the whole
and the reaction of such substitution or symbolization is a process of
"pre-logical" thinking whose effect is "sensual-emotional."[47] Although

they are miles apart in the complexity of their analysis, it is interesting to note that both Lindsay and Eisenstein hold to the same
basic belief that the substitution of the part for the whole, or objects
for actors, can often have far greater impact than the whole itself.
The primary difference between the two theorists is in their opinion of
the way the viewer learns to appreciate the symbolic technique of the
film. Lindsay contends that because of the continued use of inanimate
objects as symbols, the viewer has been trained to <u>expect</u> their use.
Eisenstein, on the other hand, insists that our appreciation of the
process of substitution derives not from any sort of conditioning, but
from archetypal patterns within the human organism.[48] While Lindsay
recognizes the pervasiveness of symbolic expression in the film, his
suggestions for its use are clouded by visionary thinking which leads
him to invest his own hieroglyphics with a multitude of highly subjective
interpretations. Again Lindsay has an intuitive understanding of the
process, but does not really come to grips with the formal problem of
symbolism. Rather, he much prefers to speculate about the social effects
of symbolic expression.

Requisite to an appreciation of the way film works is an understanding of the difference between actual and filmic time and space.
We know, for instance, that our existence in time and space is continuous; time is unbroken and inevitably moves forward. Space too, is unbroken and there is no way that we can avoid traveling <u>through</u> space.
In film, however, neither time nor space is immutable. The formal
structure of film allows time and space either to be extended or com-
pressed. Events occuring simultaneously in time but separated in space

can be depicted. Time can move either backward or forward. Only in the individual sequence is film bound by the laws of actual time and space. The concept of time and space is then one which must be understood and discussed if a theorist chooses to treat the formative principles of the motion picture. For this reason, all theorists discuss the principle, and for this reason, it is diffi.ult to isolate a particular theorist whose ideas on space and time most resembles Lindsay's. Admittedly, Lindsay's discussion of the concept is brief, but even in his one single example he seems to grasp the basic elements of the process. Time and space are, of course, functions of the editing process, but Lindsay steadfastly refuses to use the term editing with reference to the way in which time and space can be manipulated. Lindsay does not discuss in detail, the formative principles involved in the time-space concept, but, as in the case of the hieroglyphic idea, he chooses to discuss the effect of the process. To a degree, Munsterberg's discussion of time and space takes a similar approach in that he too treats the concept from a perceptual standpoint. That is, he relates the extension and the condensation of time and space to the psychological faculties of memory and imagination. Memory is associated with the "cut-back" and imagination with the "cut-forward." But here the similarity between the two ends because Munsterberg's analysis is far more detailed and better documented than Lindsay's.[49] Later theorists, of course, produced analysis of time and space as a purely formal device, which were far superior to Lindsay's. In the opinion of this writer, the clearest, most meaningful formal analysis of the time-space continuum can be found in Rudolf Arnheim's work.[50] It should also be noted that Lindsay's

discussion of time as a compositional construct is quite similar to
Eisenstein's theories of composition.[51]

Another facet of film form which derives form the editing process
is the matter of syntax, or the arrangement of the individual parts into
a meaningful whole. Lindsay, we know, believed that a properly structured film was comparable, syntactically, to a piece of prose. It was,
as he put it, a "new style of picture writing."[52] Furthermore, Lindsay
believed that this "syntactical" arrangement in the film was a firmly
established part of film technique which had conditioned the viewer to
a new kind of seeing. This new form of seeing was of great social
potential because it served as a guide for the meaningful arrangement of
the multitude of pictures which were a part of the new visual culture
which Lindsay foresaw. Bela Belazs in his film theory also foresees a
new visual culture arising from the influence of the film. Like Lindsay, Belazs contends that we are learning to see in a new way because of
the new film language. But as has been the case throughout our
comparison of Lindsay with other theorists, Balazs' discussion of the
syntax of film is far more thorough and concrete than Lindsay's.
Belazs actually refers to this new film language as a product of editing,
whereas Lindsay merely leaves it to the reader to infer that he is
speaking of editing. It should be made clear that although there are
similarities in Lindsay's and Belazs' concepts of visual culture, there
is also a difference. When Lindsay speaks of a new visual culture
developing in America, he is refering to the comprehensive visual
changes taking place in the entire country--the proliferation of newspapers, magazines, cartoons, advertisements, billboards, neon signs,

etc. Belazs, on the other hand, uses the term visual culture only to refer to a new kind of "film language."[53]

In a effort to place Lindsay's theory in the context of a long line of film theorists, we have compared his ideas with selected theorists. As would be expected, we have seen that the ideas proposed by Lindsay were analyzed by later theorists, but in much more detail. We have seen too that never is there a one to one relationship between Lindsay's theoretical concepts and those of his fellow theorists. However, beginning with Lindsay there is one unifying element which links all of the theorists we have treated. They all agree that film has unique formative capabilities which separate it from other media of expression and also make it an art in its own right. In 1915, Lindsay said that the best film makers will be those "who emphasize the points wherein the photoplay is unique. [Because], what is adapted to complete expression in one art generally secures but half expression in another."[54] One year later, Munsterberg proposed the same idea when he suggested that because of the formative elements of space, time, causality, the close-up and editing, the film is able to overcome and escape from the same forms of the "outer world."[55] Finally, to complete the circle of early theorists whom we have considered, Victor O. Freeburg sets down his views on the formative aspects of film on the first page of his book of theory. Like his predecessors, Freeburg insists that what appear to be limitations of respective arts are, in fact, the very things which differentiate among the different arts. Hence film, because of its admitted limitations and because of its peculiar assets, distinguishes itself as an art.[56] If we turn to the later theorists, we find that

they too believe that the unique formal character of the film distinguishes it as an art. Rudolf Arnheim, in a Gestalt analysis of the film
written fifteen years after Freeburg's book, summarizes the formative
means of the film by using almost the same words as does Freeburg.
Arnheim says: "What might be called the 'drawbacks' of film technique. . . actually form the tools of the creative artist."[57] It is
upon this premise that Arnheim bases his entire analysis of the formative principles of film. In the same manner, Siegfried Kracauer, bases
his entire theory of film on an assumption which sounds much like the
words written by Lindsay forty-five years earlier. Kracauer says:
"This study rests upon the assumption that each medium has a specific
nature which invites certain kinds of communications while obstructing
others."[58] It is obvious that Lindsay is the beginning of a long line
of theorists who fully understand the formal assets and liabilities of
the film, and who maintain that it is this very system of structural
checks and balances which distinguishes film as an art form.

Throughout this discussion, we have noted that in almost every
instance Lindsay's theories, when compared with others, have been
found lacking in complete development. At times, Lindsay appears to
work from intuition rather than reasoned observation. Seldom does he
pursue a theoretical idea to its logical conclusion. Ideas are not
often summarized. Seldom does he give more than one example of the idea,
and even this one example is often so extended, so thoroughly enveloped
in Lindsay's soaring mysticism, and visionary flights, that its real
meaning is clouded. Although it may sound flippant, Lindsay's own term
describes him best. He is a "theorist in motion" in the sense that he

never stands still long enough for a reader to get him in his sights.
To understand Lindsay, one is forced to follow him down a meandering
road beset with irrelevancies, bits of mysticism and highly subjective
interpretations. It is not an easy road, but it is a rewarding one, for
underneath the patina of evangelism and poetic vision are the germinal
ideals of an extremely sound theory of film. The reason for the problem
of unraveling Lindsay's theoretical ideas is best explained by Lindsay's
own assessment of The Art of the Moving Picture. In a letter to Jane
Addams, Lindsay says of the book: "It is my Hull House on paper as it
were. I was determined to put everything I thought about this whole
wide world into it, and I think I did. And then the question was so
big it was like trying to fill the ocean with one river."[59]

Clearly, Lindsay lacked the analytical powers of some of the later
theorists. Even with this limitation, Lindsay still must be regarded as
a perceptive individual who saw, at a very early stage in the development of the film, the unique formal and social powers of a new art form.
To say that Lindsay's theory is inadequate, analytically, is not
necessarily an indictment of the man who formulated the theory. It
simply says that the theory is immature. It must be also remembered
that the art was immature. In good conscience, some concessions must
be allowed for a pioneer work. If one is breaking new theoretical
ground, certain inadequacies are allowable.

There can be no doubt that Lindsay's analysis of the film was a
labor of love nurtured by a love of the traditional arts, by a love of
anything and everything visual, by a love for the elevating power of
beauty, and by no means least, by a genuine love for his fellow man.

His love for the traditional arts allows him to foresee a Michaelangelo
of film; his love for visual expression in any form allows him to foresee a new visual culture developing in which the film will be the guid-
ing force; his evangelistic devotion to beauty allows him to compare the
cowboy of the cheapest Western and the Ethopian guard of the blatantly
fantastic Arabian nights tale with the Venus de Milo and the Winged
Victory; and his love for his fellow man, the dominating influence upon
Lindsay's theory, prompts him to hope that the film can lead even the
commonest of men "through every phase of life to the apocalyptic splen-
dors."[60]

NOTES

[1] Henry M. Robinson, "The Ordeal of Vachel Lindsay," Bookman, 75 (April 1932), p. 7.

[2] Lindsay, "The Greatest. . . ," p. 90.

[3] Lindsay, The Art. . . , p. 272.

[4] Lindsay, "A Plea for the Art World," Moving Picture World, 33 (July 21, 1917), p. 368.

[5] Ibid.

[6] Lindsay, The Art. . . , pp. 270-271.

[7] Ibid., p. 225.

[8] Ibid., p. 224.

[9] Lindsay is undecided as to whether or not the structure of the film demands that the viewer learn a "new way of seeing" before he fully can comprehend what he sees. While insisting that the film can communicate with all strata of society regardless of intelligence, he also suggests that the older person with "hard, fixed, unadjustable" eyes finds it difficult to understand the "language" of the film. Nonetheless, he contends that anyone, even a young child, can learn the language of the film very quickly and easily ("The Greatest. . . ," p. 120). From Lindsay's remarks, one is left with the impression that he recognizes the unique formal structure of the film, but at the same time believes that learning to read a written language is far more difficult than learning to understand the visual language of the film. The uncertainty with which Lindsay approaches the idea of film literacy is certainly not unique. Even today, the point is still being argued. Speaking only of the difference between verbal and non-verbal communication, Susanne Langer argues that pictures are presentational and lack the subject-predicate relationship which discursive language has. See her chapter on "Discursive and Presentational Forms" (Philosophy in a New Key [New York: New American Library, 1961]). In his comparison of film and the novel, George Bluestone insists that the film is based upon perception and the novel upon conception. He says: "A film is not thought; it is perceived," whereas the novel is conceived (Novels into Film [Berkeley: University of California Press, 1961]), p. 48. Thus, the fundamental processes by which we comprehend film and novel are different. More directly to the point of Lindsay's idea of film language, however, is Sergei Eisenstein's concept of montage, in which he actually discusses the arrangement of the individual parts of the film into a meaningful,

syntatical whole (<u>Film</u> <u>Form</u>, <u>passim</u>).

[10]Letter to Louis Untermeyer, September 22, 1915, quoted in Scouffas, "Retreat and Repudiation. . . ," p. 109.

[11]Lindsay, "The Greatest. . . ," p. 90.

[12]<u>Ibid</u>., p. 22.

[13]<u>Ibid</u>., p. 23.

[14]<u>Ibid</u>., p. 24.

[15]<u>Ibid</u>.

[16]<u>Ibid</u>., p. 23.

[17]<u>Ibid</u>., p. 24.

[18]<u>Ibid</u>.

[19]<u>Ibid</u>., p. 25

[20]<u>Ibid</u>.

[21]<u>Ibid</u>., p. 23.

[22]<u>Ibid</u>., p. 120.

[23]Lindsay, <u>Collected Poems</u>, p. 1.

[24]<u>Ibid</u>., p. xvii.

[25]<u>Ibid</u>., p. xxiii.

[26]<u>Ibid</u>., p. 17.

[27]Marguerite Wilkenson, <u>New Voices: An Introduction to Contemporary Poetry</u> (New York: The Macmillan Company, 1919, p. 88.

[28]Lindsay, <u>The Art. . .</u> , p. 239.

[29] Ibid., p. 240.

[30] Conrad Aiken, Scepticisms (New York: Alfred A. Knopf, 1919, p. 156.

[31] Lindsay, Collected Poems, pp. 1-24.

[32] Ibid., p. xivi.

[33] Harriet Monroe, "Notes and Queries from Mr. Lindsay," Poetry, 17 (February, 1921), p. 264.

[34] Ibid.

[35] Letter to Eric Posselt, June 19, 1928, Barrett Collection.

[36] Ibid.

[37] Quoted in Masters, Vachel Lindsay. . . , p. 257.

[38] Lindsay, The Art. . . , p. 283-284.

[39] Rockwell Kent, This is My Own (New York: Duell, Sloan, and Pearce, 1940), pp. 13-14.

[40] Louis H. Sullivan, Kindergarten Chats (New York: Wittenborn and Schultz, Inc., 1947), passim.

[41] Ibid., p. 39.

[42] Freeburg, Pictorial Beauty. . . .

[43] Freeburg, Photoplay Making. . . , p. 27.

[44] Ibid., p. 3.

[45] Munsterberg, The Photoplay. . . , p. 52.

[46] Freeburg, Photoplay Making. . . , p. 113.

[47] Eisenstein, Film Form, p. 132.

[48]Ibid., pp. 131-133.

[49]Munsterberg, The Photoplay. . . , pp. 92-111.

[50]Rudolf Arnheim, Film As Art (Berkeley: University of California Press, 1958), pp. 20-30.

[51]Supra, p. 134.

[52]Lindsay, "The Greatest. . . ," p. 25.

[53]Bela Belazs, Theory of Film, trans. Edith Bone (London: Dennis Dobson, Ltd.), 1952, pp. 33-45.

[54]Lindsay, The Art. . . , p. 169.

[55]Munsterberg, The Photoplay. . . , p. 173.

[56]Freeburg, Photoplay Making. . . , p. 1.

[57]Arnheim, Film As Art, p. 127.

[58]Siegfried Kracauer, Theory of Film (New York: Oxford University Press, 1960), p. 3.

[59]Letter to Jane Addams, October 29, 1915, Swarthmore College Peace Collection.

[60]Lindsay, The Art. . . , p. 263.

A SELECTED BIBLIOGRAPHY

This bibliography contains materials directly refered to in the
text and sources which the writer found particularly valuable. It is
not, however, an exhaustive listing of all sources consulted.

Books

Aiken, Conrad. Scepticism: Notes on Contemporary Poetry. New York:
    Alfred A. Knopf, 1919.

Armstrong, A. Joseph (ed.). Letters of Nicholas Vachel Lindsay to
    A. Joseph Armstrong. Waco, Texas: Baylor University Press,
    1940.

Arnheim, Rudolpf. Film As Art. Berkeley: University of California
    Press, 1958.

Balazs, Bela. Theory of Film. Translated by Edith Bone. New York:
    Oxford University Press, 1960.

Baur, John I.H. Revolution and Tradition in Modern American Art.
    Cambridge: Harvard University Press, 1951.

Bluestone, George, Novels into Film. Berkeley: University of
    California Press, 1961.

Brenner, Rica. Poets of Our Time. New York: Harcourt, Brace and
    Company, 1941.

Brown, Milton. American Painting from the Armory Show to the Depression.
    Princeton: Princeton University Press, 1955.

Davidson, Edward. Some Modern Poets. New York: Harper and Brothers,
    1928.

Eisenstein, Sergei. Film Form. Translated by Jay Leyda. New York:
    Meridian Books, Inc., 1949.

Freeburg, Victor O. The Art of Photoplay Making. New York: The
    Macmillan Company, 1918.

_____. Pictorial Beauty on the Screen. New York: The Macmillan
    Company, 1923.

Garrison, Winfred Earnest and DeGroot, Alfred T. The Disciples of
    Christ: A History. St. Louis: Christian Board of
    Publication, 1948.

Graham, Steven. Tramping with A poet in the Rockies. New York: D.
    Appleton and Company, 1922.

Hicks, John D. The Populist Revolt. Minneapolis: University of
    Minnesota Press, 1931.

Humbert, Royal (ed.) A Compend of Alexander Campbell's Theology. St.
    Louis: Bethany Press, 1961.

Kent, Rockwell. This Is My Own. New York: Duell, Sloan and Pearce,
    1940.

Kracauer, Siegfried. Theory of Film. New York: Oxford University
    Press, 1960.

Langer, Susanne K. Philosophy in a New Key. New York: New American
    Library, 1961.

Lindsay, Nicholas Vachel. Adventures While Preaching the Gospel of
    Beauty. New York: The Macmillan Company, 1928.

_____. The Art of the Moving Picture. First ed. New York: The
    Macmillan Company, 1916.

_____. The Art of the Moving Picture. Second ed. rev. New York: The
    Macmillan Company, 1922.

_____. Collected Poems. New York: The Macmillan Company, 1926.

_____. A Handy Guide For Beggars. New York: The Macmillan Company,
    1916.

Masters, Edgar Lee. Vachel Lindsay: A Poet in America. New York:
    Charles Scribner's Sons, 1935.

Munsterberg, Hugo. The Photoplay: A Psychological Study. New York:
    D. Appleton and Company, 1916.

Sullivan, Louis H. Kindergarten Chats. New York: Wittenborn, Schultz,
    Inc., 1947.

Toksvig, Signe. Emanuel Swedenborg: Scientist and Mystic. New Haven:
    Yale University Press, 1948.

Trobridge, George. Swedenborg: Life and Teaching. New York: Sweden-
    borg Foundation, 1944.

Trombly, Albert Edmund. Vachel Lindsay, Adventurer. Columbia, Missouri:
    Lucas Brothers, 1929.

Untermeyer, Louis. The New Era In American Poetry. New York: Henry
    Holt and Company, 1919.

Wilkinson, Marguerite. <u>New</u> <u>Voices</u>: An <u>Introduction</u> <u>to</u> <u>Contemporary</u>
<u>Poetry</u>. New York: The Macmillan Company, 1919.

Yatron, Michael. <u>America's</u> <u>Literary</u> <u>Revolt</u>. New York: Philosophical
Library, 1959.

Periodicals

Betts, Ernest. "The Film as Literature," <u>Saturday</u> <u>Review</u> (London), 144
(December 31, 1927), p. 905.

Emerson, John and Loos, Anita. "Photoplay Writing," <u>Photoplay</u>, 24
(June 1918), p. 78.

Hackett, Francis. "The Poet at the Movies," <u>New</u> <u>Republic</u>, V (December
25, 1915), pp. 201-202.

Holt, Edgar. "Vachel Lindsay 'Poet and Pioneer of Cinema,'" <u>Bookman</u>
(London), VII (January 1932), p. 244.

Jones, Llewellyn. "Vachel Lindsay: American Poet," <u>Christian</u> <u>Century</u>,
48 (December 23, 1931), pp. 1619-1620.

Lindsay, Vachel. "Back Your Train Up To My Pony," <u>New</u> <u>Republic</u>, X
(March 10, 1917), pp. 166-167.

_____. "The Great Douglas Fairbanks," <u>Ladies</u> <u>Home</u> <u>Journal</u>, August
1926.

_____. "The Movies," <u>New</u> <u>Republic</u>, IX (January 13, 1917), pp. 302-
303.

_____. "Photoplay Progress," <u>New</u> <u>Republic</u>, 10 (February 17, 1917),
pp. 76-77.

_____. "A Plea for the Art World," <u>Moving</u> <u>Picture</u> <u>World</u>, 33 (July 21,
1917), p. 368.

_____. "Queen of My People," <u>New</u> <u>Republic</u>, XI (July 7, 1917), pp.
280-281.

_____. "Venus in Armor," <u>New</u> <u>Republic</u>, X (March 28, 1917), pp. 380-
381.

Loos, Anita. "Vachel, Mae and I," <u>Saturday</u> <u>Review</u>, August 26, 1961.

Luquiens, H-M. "The Art of the Moving Picture," <u>The</u> <u>Yale</u> <u>Review</u>, V
(July 1916), p. 896.

MacFarlane, Peter C. "Vagabond Poet," <u>Colliers</u>, 51 (September 6, 1913), pp. 7-8.

Manvell, Roger. "A Forgotten Critic," <u>Sight</u> <u>and</u> <u>Sound</u>, Spring and Winter 1949-1950, p. 76.

Masters, Edgar Lee. "Vachel Lindsay and America," <u>Saturday</u> <u>Review</u> <u>of</u> <u>Literature,</u> 12 (August 10, 1935), p. 3.

Monroe, Harriet. "The Liminal Lindsay," <u>Poetry</u>, 29 (January 1927), pp. 217-221.

_____. "Notes and Queries From Mr. Lindsay," <u>Poetry</u> 17 (February, 1921), pp. 262-266.

_____. "Vachel Lindsay," <u>Poetry</u>, 24 (May 1924), pp. 90-95.

Thalinger, T.W. "Vachel Lindsay: Pen and Ink Symbolist," <u>Magazine</u> <u>of</u> <u>Art</u>, 31 (August 1938), pp. 450-456.

Robinson, Henry M. "The Ordeal of Vachel Lindsay," <u>Bookman</u> (London), 75 (April 1932), pp. 6-9.

"Vachel Lindsay on Film," <u>Image</u>, II (April 1953), p. 23.

Manuscripts

Cockerell, Dura B. "Vachel Lindsay, Artist." Manuscript, Lindsay-Cockerell Collection, Illinois State Historical Library, Springfield, Illinois, n.d.

Lindsay, Vachel. "Blue Four Review." Manuscript, The Barrett Collection, University of Virginia Library, Charlottesville, Virginia, n. d.

_____. "Charter Copy." Manuscript, The Barrett Collection, University of Virginia Library, Charlottesville, Virginia, n. d.

_____. "The Greatest Movies Now Running." The Barrett Collection, University of Virginia Library, Charlottesville, Virginia <u>ca</u>. 1925.

_____. "Sound Is the Servant-Not the Master of the Camera." Manuscript, The Barrett Collection, University of Virginia, Charlottesville, Virginia, ca. 1927.

_____. "A Special Delivery Letter to My Particular Friends." Manu-
script, The Barrett Collection, University of Virginia
Library, Charlottesville, Virginia, file dated 1925-1929.

_____. "The Vitaphone." Manuscript, the Barrett Collection, Uni-
versity of Virginia Library, Charlottesville, Virginia, <u>ca</u>.
1927.

_____. "Why I Think Douglas Fairbanks is a Great Man." Manuscript,
The Barrett Collection, University of Virginia Library,
Charlottesville, Virginia, 1926.

Unpublished Dissertations

Heffernan, Miriam Margaret. "The Ideas and Methods of Vachel Lindsay."
Ph. D. dissertation, New York University, New York City, New
York, 1948.

Kuydendall, Radford B. "The Reading and Speaking of Vachel Lindsay."
Ph. D. dissertation, Northwestern University, Evanston,
Illinois, 1952.

Scouffas, George. "Vachel Lindsay: A Study in Retreat and Repudiation."
Ph. D. dissertation, University of Illinois, Urbana, Illinois,
1951.

Letters

Letter to Dr. Vachel Lindsay. November 3, 1903. The Barrett Collection,
University of Virginia Library, Charlottesville, Virginia.

Letter to Dr. and Mrs. Vachel Lindsay. November 10, 1903. Barrett
Collection, University of Virginia Library, Charlottesville,
Virginia.

Letter to Dr. Vachel Lindsay. November 14, 1903. The Barrett Collection. University of Virginia Library, Charlottesville,
Virginia.

Letter to Mrs. Vachel Lindsay. January 31, 1904. The Barrett Collection, University of Virginia Library, Charlottesville,
Virginia.

Letter to Mrs. Vachel Lindsay. February 19, 1904. The Barrett Collection, University of Virginia Library Charlottesville, Virginia.

Letter to Mrs. Vachel Lindsay. March 16, 1904. The Barrett Collection,
University of Virginia Library, Charlottesville, Virginia.

Letter to Mrs. Vachel Lindsay. March 17, 1904. The Barrett Collection, University of Virginia Library, Charlottesville, Virginia.

Letter to Mrs. Vachel Lindsay. April 2, 1904. The Barrett Collection, University of Virginia Library, Charlottesville, Virginia.

Letter to Louis Untermeyer. September 22, 1915. Quoted in Scouffas, George. "Vachel Lindsay: A Study in Retreat and Repudiation," Unpublished Ph. D. dissertation, University of Illinois, Urbana, Illinois, 1951.

Letter to Harriet Monroe. October 12, 1916. Quoted in Kuykendall, Radford B. "The Reading and Speaking of Vachel Lindsay." Unpublished Ph.D. dissertation, Northwestern University, Evanston, Illinois, 1952.

Letter to Jane Addams. October 15, 1916. Jane Addams Collection, Swarthmore College Peace Collection, Swarthmore, Pennsylvania.

Letter to Jane Addams. October 29, 1916. Jane Addams Collection, Swarthmore College Peace Collection, Swarthmore, Pennsylvania.

Letter to Harriet Monroe. January 12, 1917. Quoted in Kuykendall, Radford B. "The Reading and Speaking of Vachel Lindsay." Unpublished Ph. D. dissertation, Northwestern University, Evanston, Illinois, 1952.

Letter from Mary Pickford. September 10, 1924. The Barrett Collection, University of Virginia Library, Charlottesville, Virginia.

Letter to Professor Harold L. Bruce. January 17, 1925. The Barrett Collection, University of Virginia Library, Charlottesville, Virginia.

Letter to John Drinkwater. February 16, 1925. The Barrett Collection, University of Virginia Library, Charlottesville, Virginia.

Letter from Edgar Lee Masters. November 8, 1925. The Barrett Collection, University of Virginia Library, Charlottesville, Virginia.

Letter to Marguerite Wilkinson, July 4, 1927. The Lindsay-Cockerell Collection, Illinois State Historical Library, Springfield, Illinois.

Letter to Burris A. Jenkins. July 12, 1927. The Lindsay-Cockerell Collection, Illinois State Historical Library, Springfield, Illinois.

Letter to Eric Posselt. June 19, 1928. The Barrett Collection, University of Virginia Library, Charlottesville, Virginia.

Letter to the author from Eileen Bowser, Curator of Films, Museum of
    Modern Art, New York City, New York. February 26, 1964.

Letter from Isadora Bennett Reed. Quoted in Kuykendall, Radford B.
    "The Reading and Speaking of Vachel Lindsay." Unpublished
    Ph. D. dissertation, Northwestern University, Evanston,
    Illinois, 1952.

Miscellaneous--from Lindsay's personal papers

Annual Statement of Royalty Account. The Macmillan Company. July 29,
    1924. Barrett Collection, University of Virginia,
    Charlottesville, Virginia.

Broadside. Lindsay, Vachel. The Gospel of Beauty. 1912. Barrett
    Collection, University of Virginia Library, Charlottesville,
    Virginia.

Lindsay, Vachel. "Poem Games For All the World." "The Vitaphone."
    Unpublished manuscript, The Barrett Collection, University of
    Virginia Library, Charlottesville, Virginia, c. 1927.

Personal Diary. January 3, 1905. The Barrett Collection, University of
    Virginia Library, Charlottesville, Virginia.

Personal Diary. May 6, 1922. The Barrett Collection, University of
    Virginia Library, Charlottesville, Virginia.

Personal Notebook. July 20, 1907. The Barrett Collection, University
    of Virginia Library, Charlottesville, Virginia.

Personal Notebook. June 2, 1924. The Barrett Collection, University
    of Virginia Library, Charlottesville, Virginia.

Personal Notebook. February 5, 1925. The Barrett Collection, Uni-
    versity of Virginia Library, Charlottesville, Virginia.

Personal Notebook. February 12, 1926. The Barrett Collection, Uni-
    versity of Virginia Library, Charlottesville, Virginia.

Personal notebook, n. d. The Barrett Collection,University of Virginia
    Library, Charlottesville, Virginia.

Press clipping. Illinois State Register. Springfield, Illinois,
    December 15, 1910. The Barrett Collection, University of
    Virginia Library, Charlottesville, Virginia.

Press clipping. "The Necessity of Reverence." Unknown Springfield, Illinois newspaper, n. d. The Barrett Collection, University of Virginia Library, Charlottesville, Virginia.

Promotional Flyer. "About Vachel Lindsay's Books." William E. Feakins Inc. n. d. The Barrett Collection, University of Virginia Library, Charlottesville, Virginia.

Promotional Flyer. Lindsay, Vachel. "A Letter About My Four Programmes." 1916. The Barrett Collection, University of Virginia Library, Charlottesville, Virginia.

Promotional Flyer. Lindsay Mrs. 1925-1929. The Barrett Collection, University of Virginia Library, Charlottesville, Virginia.

Promotional Flyer. "Vachel Lindsay, Troubadour." William E. Feakins Inc., n. d. The Barrett Collection, University of Virginia Library, Charlottesville, Virginia.

The Arno Press Cinema Program

THE LITERATURE OF CINEMA

Series I & II

Agate, James. **Around Cinemas.** 1946.

Agate, James. **Around Cinemas.** (Second Series). 1948.

American Academy of Political and Social Science. **The Motion Picture in Its Economic and Social Aspects,** edited by Clyde L. King. **The Motion Picture Industry,** edited by Gordon S. Watkins. *The Annals,* November, 1926/1927.

L'Art Cinematographique, Nos. 1-8. 1926-1931.

Balcon, Michael, Ernest Lindgren, Forsyth Hardy and Roger Manvell. **Twenty Years of British Film, 1925-1945.** 1947.

Bardèche, Maurice and Robert Brasillach. **The History of Motion Pictures,** edited by Iris Barry. 1938.

Benoit-Levy, Jean. **The Art of the Motion Picture.** 1946.

Blumer, Herbert. **Movies and Conduct.** 1933.

Blumer, Herbert and Philip M. Hauser. **Movies, Delinquency, and Crime.** 1933.

Buckle, Gerard Fort. **The Mind and the Film.** 1926.

Carter, Huntly. **The New Spirit in the Cinema.** 1930.

Carter, Huntly. **The New Spirit in the Russian Theatre, 1917-1928.** 1929.

Carter, Huntly. **The New Theatre and Cinema of Soviet Russia.** 1924.

Charters, W. W. **Motion Pictures and Youth.** 1933.

Cinema Commission of Inquiry. **The Cinema: Its Present Position and Future Possibilities.** 1917.

Dale, Edgar. **Children's Attendance at Motion Pictures.** Dysinger, Wendell S. and Christian A. Ruckmick. **The Emotional Responses of Children to the Motion Picture Situation.** 1935.

Dale, Edgar. **The Content of Motion Pictures.** 1935.

Dale, Edgar. **How to Appreciate Motion Pictures.** 1937.

Dale, Edgar, Fannie W. Dunn, Charles F. Hoban, Jr., and Etta Schneider. **Motion Pictures in Education: A Summary of the Literature.** 1938.

Davy, Charles. **Footnotes to the Film.** 1938.

Dickinson, Thorold and Catherine De la Roche. **Soviet Cinema.** 1948.

Dickson, W. K. L., and Antonia Dickson. **History of the Kinetograph, Kinetoscope and Kinetophonograph.** 1895.

Forman, Henry James. **Our Movie Made Children.** 1935.

Freeburg, Victor Oscar. **The Art of Photoplay Making.** 1918.

Freeburg, Victor Oscar. **Pictorial Beauty on the Screen.** 1923.

Hall, Hal, editor. **Cinematographic Annual,** 2 vols. 1930/1931.

Hampton, Benjamin B. **A History of the Movies.** 1931.

Hardy, Forsyth. **Scandinavian Film.** 1952.

Hepworth, Cecil M. **Animated Photography: The A B C of the Cinematograph.** 1900.

Hoban, Charles F., Jr., and Edward B. Van Ormer. **Instructional Film Research 1918-1950.** 1950.

Holaday, Perry W. and George D. Stoddard. **Getting Ideas from the Movies.** 1933.

Hopwood, Henry V. **Living Pictures.** 1899.

Hulfish, David S. **Motion-Picture Work.** 1915.

Hunter, William. **Scrutiny of Cinema.** 1932.

Huntley, John. **British Film Music.** 1948.

Irwin, Will. **The House That Shadows Built.** 1928.

Jarratt, Vernon. **The Italian Cinema.** 1951.

Jenkins, C. Francis. **Animated Pictures.** 1898.

Lang, Edith and George West. **Musical Accompaniment of Moving Pictures.** 1920.

London, Kurt. **Film Music.** 1936.

Lutz, E[dwin] G [eorge]. **The Motion-Picture Cameraman.** 1927.

Manvell, Roger. **Experiment in the Film.** 1949.

Marey, Etienne Jules. **Movement.** 1895.

Martin, Olga J. **Hollywood's Movie Commandments.** 1937.

Mayer, J. P. **Sociology of Film: Studies and Documents.** 1946. New Introduction by J. P. Mayer.

Münsterberg, Hugo. **The Photoplay: A Psychological Study.** 1916.

Nicoll, Allardyce. **Film and Theatre.** 1936.

Noble, Peter. **The Negro in Films.** 1949.

Peters, Charles C. **Motion Pictures and Standards of Morality.** 1933.

Peterson, Ruth C. and L. L. Thurstone. **Motion Pictures and the Social Attitudes of Children.** Shuttleworth, Frank K. and Mark A. May. **The Social Conduct and Attitudes of Movie Fans.** 1933.

Phillips, Henry Albert. **The Photodrama.** 1914.

Photoplay Research Society. **Opportunities in the Motion Picture Industry.** 1922.

Rapée, Erno. **Encyclopaedia of Music for Pictures.** 1925.

Rapée, Erno. **Motion Picture Moods for Pianists and Organists.** 1924.

Renshaw, Samuel, Vernon L. Miller and Dorothy P. Marquis. **Children's Sleep.** 1933.

Rosten, Leo C. Hollywood: The Movie Colony, The Movie Makers. 1941.

Sadoul, Georges. French Film. 1953.

Screen Monographs I, 1923-1937. 1970.

Screen Monographs II, 1915-1930. 1970.

Sinclair, Upton. Upton Sinclair Presents William Fox. 1933.

Talbot, Frederick A. Moving Pictures. 1912.

Thorp, Margaret Farrand. America at the Movies. 1939.

Wollenberg, H. H. Fifty Years of German Film. 1948.

RELATED BOOKS AND PERIODICALS

Allister, Ray. Friese-Greene: Close-Up of an Inventor. 1948.

Art in Cinema: A Symposium of the Avant-Garde Film, edited by Frank Stauffacher. 1947.

The Art of Cinema: Selected Essays. New Foreword by George Amberg. 1971.

Balázs, Béla. Theory of the Film. 1952.

Barry, Iris. Let's Go to the Movies. 1926.

de Beauvoir, Simone. Brigitte Bardot and the Lolita Syndrome. 1960.

Carrick, Edward. Art and Design in the British Film. 1948.

Close Up. Vols. 1-10, 1927-1933 (all published).

Cogley, John. Report on Blacklisting. Part I: The Movies. 1956.

Eisenstein, S. M. Que Viva Mexico! 1951.

Experimental Cinema. 1930-1934 (all published).

Feldman, Joseph and Harry. Dynamics of the Film. 1952.

Film Daily Yearbook of Motion Pictures. Microfilm, 18 reels, 35 mm. 1918-1969.

Film Daily Yearbook of Motion Pictures. 1970.

Film Daily Yearbook of Motion Pictures. (Wid's Year Book). 3 vols., 1918-1922.

The Film Index: A Bibliography. Vol. I: The Film as Art. 1941.

Film Society Programmes. 1925-1939 (all published).

Films: A Quarterly of Discussion and Analysis. Nos. 1-4, 1939-1940 (all published).

Flaherty, Frances Hubbard. The Odyssey of a Film-Maker: Robert Flaherty's Story. 1960.

General Bibliography of Motion Pictures, edited by Carl Vincent, Riccardo Redi, and Franco Venturini. 1953.

Hendricks, Gordon. Origins of the American Film. 1961-1966. New Introduction by Gordon Hendricks.

Hound and Horn: Essays on Cinema, 1928-1934. 1971.

Huff, Theodore. **Charlie Chaplin.** 1951.

Kahn, Gordon. **Hollywood on Trial.** 1948.

New York Times Film Reviews, 1913-1968. 1970.

Noble, Peter. **Hollywood Scapegoat: The Biography of Erich von Stroheim.** 1950.

Robson, E. W. and M. M. **The Film Answers Back.** 1939.

Seldes, Gilbert. **An Hour with the Movies and the Talkies.** 1929.

Weinberg, Herman G., editor. **Greed.** 1971.

Wollenberg, H. H. **Anatomy of the Film.** 1947.

Wright, Basil. **The Use of the Film.** 1948.

DISSERTATIONS ON FILM

Karpf, Stephen L. **The Gangster Film: Emergence, Variation and Decay of a Genre, 1930-1940.** First publication, 1973.

Lounsbury, Myron O. **The Origins of American Film Criticism, 1909-1939.** First publication, 1973.

Sands, Pierre N. **A Historical Study of the Academy of the Motion Picture Arts and Sciences (1927-1947).** First publication, 1973.

North, Joseph H. **The Early Development of the Motion Picture, 1887-1909.** First publication, 1973.

Rimberg, John. **The Motion Picture in the Soviet Union, 1918-1952.** First publication, 1973.

Wolfe, Glenn J. **Vachel Lindsay: The Poet as Film Theorist.** First publication, 1973.